MW00451902

THE TEACHING FOR SOCIAL JUSTICE SERIES

William Ayers—*Series Editor*   **Therese Quinn**—*Associate Series Editor*

Teacher Educators as Critical Storytellers

Effective Teachers as Windows and Mirrors

EDITED BY

Antonio L. Ellis
Nicholas D. Hartlep
Gloria Ladson-Billings
David O. Stovall

FOREWORD BY
LESLIE T. FENWICK

AFTERWORD BY
DAWN G. WILLIAMS

TEACHERS COLLEGE PRESS

TEACHERS COLLEGE | COLUMBIA UNIVERSITY
NEW YORK AND LONDON

Published by Teachers College Press,® 1234 Amsterdam Avenue, New York, NY 10027

Front cover photo by SDI Productions / iStock by Getty Images.

Library of Congress Cataloging-in-Publication Data

Names: Ellis, Antonio L., editor. | Hartlep, Nicholas Daniel, editor. |
   Ladson-Billings, Gloria, 1947– editor. | Stovall, David, editor. |
   Fenwick, Leslie T., writer of foreword. | Williams, Dawn (Dawn G.),
   writer of afterword.
Title: Teacher educators as critical storytellers : effective teachers as
   windows and mirrors / edited by Antonio L. Ellis, Nicholas D. Hartlep,
   Gloria Ladson-Billings, David O. Stovall ; foreword by Leslie T. Fenwick
   ; afterword by Dawn Williams.
Description: New York : Teachers College Press, [2021] | Series: Teaching
   for social justice series | Includes bibliographical references and
   index.
Identifiers: LCCN 2020051752 (print) | LCCN 2020051753 (ebook) | ISBN
   9780807765159 (Hardcover : acid-free paper) | ISBN 9780807765142
   (Paperback : acid-free paper) | ISBN 9780807779460 (eBook)
Subjects: LCSH: Teacher educators—United States—Anecdotes. |
   Teachers—Training of—United States. | Teachers—In-service
   training—United States. | Culturally relevant pedagogy—United States.
   | Social justice—Study and teaching—United States.
Classification: LCC LB1715 .T42523 2021 (print) | LCC LB1715 (ebook) |
   DDC 370.71/1—dc23
LC record available at https://lccn.loc.gov/2020051752
LC ebook record available at https://lccn.loc.gov/2020051753

ISBN 978-0-8077-6514-2 (paper)
ISBN 978-0-8077-6515-9 (hardcover)
ISBN 978-0-8077-7946-0 (ebook)

Printed on acid-free paper
Manufactured in the United States of America

This volume was conceptualized and is dedicated in honor of Mr. Linard H. McCloud, the legendary music teacher and director of bands at Burke High School in Charleston, South Carolina.

Thank you for 41-and-counting years of commitment, inspiration, and effective teaching at the same school.

The editors honor all teachers who are highlighted in the forthcoming chapters for their effectiveness in the classroom and beyond.

These teachers served as "windows and mirrors" for the students they served.

Contents

PART III: NATIVE AMERICAN PERSPECTIVES: INDIGENEITY IS NOT RACE

PART IV: LATINX PERSPECTIVES: THE LATINIZATION OF EDUCATION

Foreword

Teacher Educators as Critical Storytellers is essential reading. If you enjoy stories, you will enjoy this volume. These are no vague, ordinary stories or storytellers. These teacher-stories have the soul of a poem, the unflinching truth of a calypso song, the urgency of a solider captured behind enemy lines, and a prayer's abiding call for blessing. Each chapter offers an intimate view of what it feels like to be taught by a teacher who affirms to the student: *You belong here.*

The authors in this volume remind us of two truths. First, all students deserve and need diverse models of intellectual authority. Today, there is a yawning demographic mismatch between public school students and the educators (teachers and principals) who serve them. More than 50% of the nation's schoolchildren are kids of color. Yet less than 20% of the nation's 3.2 million teachers are educators of color. Children and adolescents do not see or experience diverse models of intellectual authority in their schools. Shockingly, nearly 40% of the nation's schools have no teacher of color. Further, the teaching force is even monolithic in urban and inner-city (central city poor communities) schools. Ninety-one percent of urban schoolteachers are White, and 73% of inner-city teachers are White.

Second, compounding the demographic mismatch between schoolchildren and educators is the problem with the authorship, content, and imagery of K–12 school textbooks. Each is almost exclusively White and does not reflect a true and inclusive perspective about the nation's and the world's intellectual and cultural contributors and achievements. This lack of diversity in the educator workforce, textbook authorship, and even standardized test design has been deleterious to the academic progress of African American and other children of color who have been cast as intellectually inferior and culturally lacking.

In high-diversity–staffed schools certain academic and social benefits accrue to students of color, including increased reading achievement in the elementary grades and math achievement in high school, greater likelihood of graduating high school in 4 years and matriculating college, greater likelihood of being tested for and placed in gifted education, and less likelihood of being misplaced in special education and suspended or expelled from school. Additionally, teachers of color report fewer negative perceptions and attitudes toward students of color and are more likely than their White teacher peers to describe students of color as intellectually capable and engaged in school-affirming behaviors (such as attendance, homework completion, active participation, and taking a leadership role in the classroom).

Until the nation achieves its educator workforce diversity goals, how can we ensure that schools are places where all children feel they belong? The teacher-stories told here guide the way. Through them we learn that teachers who make a lasting and positive impact on their students (especially students of color) understand that teaching is about relationship building and identity restoration (personal and cultural). These memorable teachers achieve this by *being* and *acting* in the following distinct and traceable ways:

1. They have a kinship with their students and watch over them with kindness, love, and understanding. They also exude an inner strength. Therefore, students trust that their teacher protects students' well-being and best interests.
2. They create stable learning environments that are intellectually challenging and stimulating, safe and nurturing. Teaching and learning in their classrooms have a rhythm. They create rituals, traditions, and celebrations with their students to mark achievement of academic and social goals.
3. They *study* and *know* their students as much as they study and know the subject area they teach. Daily they model and act in respectful, caring, inspirational, and generative ways with their students.
4. They utilize a cultural eye and exhibit commitment to learning the language and/or cultural history of their students and utilize the students' language and/or cultural history in the subject area being taught. They understand that every student is a part of a cultural/ethnic tradition. In addition, all students exist in a political and economic environment, an environment that, for the student of color, has included harmful encounters with racism. They teach and model strategies for overcoming racism and other life obstacles. They confront the debilitating beliefs and actions associated with racism.

5. They affirm students' intellectual and other abilities and connect them to resources that enhance their capacities. They offer hope and a future.

Teacher Educators as Critical Storytellers proves what the radical 1960s
poet Haki Madhubuti told us: Good teachers don't just do, they be!

—Leslie T. Fenwick, dean in residence at the American Association of Colleges for Teacher Education (AACTE) and dean emerita of
the Howard University School of Education

Teacher Educators as Critical Storytellers

Effective Teachers as Windows and Mirrors

Effective Teachers as Windows and Mirrors

An Introduction

The editors of this volume wished to produce a book that would be useful and appealing to a diverse readership, which is why we commissioned highly influential teacher educators to contribute chapters. Our intended audience is preservice and prospective teacher education students, certified/licensed inservice teachers, teacher education scholars, researchers, policymakers, and faculty and administrators in the fields of higher education, teacher education, educational leadership, and educational policy. We hope that such readers will consult this volume in reference to their work on effective teaching practices. This book will help them identify the long-lasting impact that a teacher's race can have on the life of their students beyond high school and college graduation. We expect this volume to be "foundational," and its chapters highly cited.

The chapters of this book, collectively, push back against what Haberman (2012) labeled the "myth of the 'fully qualified' bright young teacher," which is racialized and gendered as being a White female teacher. The main problem of this single, narrow narrative is that it reinforces the antiquated notion that White females make the best teachers. This book breaks away from that historically dominant and pervasive narrative by providing readers exposure to diverse storytellers—all of whom are teacher educators. The authors address race, ethnicity, and indigeneity, as well as justice issues such as a "democratic" as opposed to a "demographic" imperative when considering who teaches and who is taught in our nation's E–12 schools (Sleeter et al., 2015). Drawing on the work of Style (1996), we contend that effective teachers serve as both "windows" and "mirrors" for students— meaning that teachers must reflect the student population in racial and cultural terms while also serving as a window for students to see opportunities that lie outside of their immediate context.

1

For instance, Ellis (2016) describes his high school music teacher, Mr. Linard McCloud, as "a highly effective African American music educator who changed the course of [his] life" (p. 170). McCloud, according to Ellis, was loving, caring, creative, culturally sensitive, attuned, hopeful, flexible, organized, and thoughtful. McCloud's teaching characteristics and dispositions motivated Ellis to achieve academically and socially in his urban high school. As an African American male, McCloud served as a "mirror" for Ellis. Moreover, McCloud was a highly effective educator because he went beyond the call of duty as a teacher—a practice that Ellis believes is not the rule in schools but more the exception. Not only did McCloud teach in the classroom setting, but he also built strong relationships with families, community members, and external stakeholders including local businesses, colleges, and universities. McCloud used these networks to leverage opportunities for his students academically, personally, and professionally. Like many of his African American high school classmates, Ellis writes about how he would not have graduated from high school if it were not for the care and mentorship he received from McCloud. McCloud simultaneously served as a "window": Ellis could see the many opportunities that existed outside of Charleston, South Carolina, that he would not have seen otherwise. Another goal of this volume is to honor teachers like McCloud who have made a difference in the lives of their students, while also learning from their effective practices by considering their roles as both "windows" and "mirrors."

Employing a "critical storytelling" methodology (see Hartlep & Hensley, 2015; Hartlep et al., 2017), each chapter contributor uses their own narrative to share the effective teaching practices of influential teachers that they have had. While this "critical storytelling" framework centers race, gender, and lived and learned experiences, the storyteller is the most important unit of analysis; hence, *Teacher Educators as Critical Storytellers: Effective Teachers as Windows and Mirrors* includes contributions from teacher educators with diverse backgrounds in terms of race, ethnicity, and indigeneity. The book includes Asian American, African American, Latinx, and Native American storytellers. It concludes by offering recommendations for preservice teachers and inservice teachers who desire to leave a lasting impact on students by serving as "windows" and "mirrors."

Keeping in alignment with Teachers College Press's Teaching for Social Justice series, chapter contributors employ a "critical storytelling" methodology to illuminate connections between their teachers' race, ethnicity, and/or indigeneity and their attitude, achievement, self-esteem, and their own current practice as teacher educators. Ellis, Hartlep, Ladson-Billings, and Stovall, the editors of this project, have been deeply influenced by one or more teachers who have served as windows and, at times, mirrors. The editors remember these teachers with fondness; tell their stories to their own students; and think of them with affection, respect, gratitude, and even reverence. Sometimes we recognized this influence as it was happening, and we grew close to these remarkable individuals, keeping them in our lives even after we graduated from their classes. Often, however, they themselves were unaware of the influence they exercised over us, for it was not until years passed that we realized their lasting effect. If time and distance did not prevent it, perhaps we found our way back to these educators and shared with them our appreciation and gratitude.

We commissioned a range of respected scholars in the fields of education (teacher education and otherwise), educational psychology, administration and policy, and curriculum and instruction to provide us with narratives describing their most memorable teacher using a race-, ethnicity-, and/or indigeneity-based lens. Each chapter includes an analysis drawn from research on identity in teacher education, theory, and research in education, psychology, and human development. Applicable key concepts and principles that explain why the selected teacher was so memorably effective are identified. These layered and multifaceted analyses serve as the book's conclusion.

It is our hope that these critical stories will be of value to preservice and inservice teachers who are engaged in the important responsibility of teaching our nation's youth. In a sense, we hope the chapters provide a series of templates that help identify the attitudes and behaviors of those teachers who make a difference in the lives of their students by serving as windows and mirrors. Of course, we believe that these stories about exceptional classroom teachers and professors will also further the mission of this critical book series.

REFERENCES

Ellis, A. L. (2016). An autoethnographic exploration of an African American male professor who stutters. In K. Cumings Mansfield, A. D. Welton, & P. Lee (Eds.), *Identity intersectionality, mentoring, and work-life (im)balance* (pp. 165–178). Information Age.

Haberman, M. (2012). The myth of the "fully qualified" bright young teacher. *American Behavioral Scientist, 56*(7), 926–940.

Hartlep, N. D., & Hensley, B. (Eds.). (2015). *Critical storytelling in uncritical times: Stories disclosed in a cultural foundations of education course.* Sense Publishers–Rotterdam.

Hartlep, N. D., Hensley, B. O., Braniger, C. J., & Jennings, M. E. (Eds.). (2017). *Critical storytelling in uncritical times: Undergraduates share their stories in higher education.* Sense Publishers–Rotterdam.

Sleeter, C. E., Neal, L. V. I., & Kumashiro, K. K. (Eds.). (2015). *Diversifying the teacher workforce: Preparing and retaining highly effective teachers.* Routledge.

Style, E. (1996). Curriculum as window and mirror. *Social Science Record.* Available for download from https://nationalseedproject.org/Key-SEED-Texts/curriculum-as-window-and-mirror

Part I

AFRICAN AMERICAN PERSPECTIVES

Toward "Demographic" and "Democratic" Imperatives

CHAPTER 1

Mr. Linard H. McCloud

A Dreamkeeper in the American Education Milieu

Antonio L. Ellis

Debates regarding the qualities, skills, and dispositions of effective teachers and teaching have raged in teacher education for several decades. Ladson-Billings's (2009) *The Dreamkeepers: Successful Teachers of African American Children* was a pathbreaking work that has become a foundational study that informs the work of "culturally relevant" (Ladson-Billings, 2009) and "culturally sustaining" (Paris & Alim, 2017) teaching. In *The Dreamkeepers*, Ladson-Billings describes effective teachers who are able to draw from the cultural wealth of Black communities. These Dreamkeepers ensured that their Black students were academically successful and grew in terms of their cultural competence as well as their sociopolitical awareness. In other words, according to Ladson-Billings (2009), these effective teachers possessed both pedagogical and relational dispositions, which leave lifelong impacts on the academic and social lives of their students. As some scholars have noted, what remains missing from the research on culturally relevant and even culturally sustaining teachers are "narratives" (that is, stories, *cuentos*, *testimonios*, and so on) related to how the race of particular K–12 teachers positively impact the lives of their students because they served as either windows or mirrors (Bryan, 2020; Howard, 2001; Irvine & Fenwick, 2011; Milner, 2011). This volume aims to help fill this gap in educational research literature.

The foundation of this volume stems from the classroom experiences provided to me by my high school music teacher. In August of 1995, I entered Burke High School in Charleston, South Carolina as an urban student who was placed in speech therapy, special education, and lower-tracked courses (Ellis & Hartlep, 2017). I lacked motivation toward education, and the majority of my teachers did not have high expectations of me. Members of my family averaged an 8th-grade education. While growing up, I was encouraged to do just enough to get by academically and in life. From my recollection, all of my family members who raised me did not complete high school. Some dropped out prior to high school. Based on my surroundings and the odds that were against me, my chances for success appeared to be extremely dismal. Many people in society gave up on me, including schoolteachers, guidance counselors, clergy, and community leaders. Eventually, I felt like all hope was lost and never imagined that I would graduate from high school.

MY EXPERIENCES AT BURKE HIGH SCHOOL

Upon entering Burke High School, I decided to seek membership in the marching band. At that time I knew very little about musical instruments. I simply thought that joining the band program would be a fun thing to do. As I reflect on the first band practice of that school year, I recall the music teacher and marching band director Linard McCloud's "pep talk." Everyone was completely silent as he talked in a very low and firm tone, explaining his expectation of all band members. He was very clear about what he expected from all students. Not only did he express his expectations of band students, he also talked about his expectations for the alumni of the band program. That was the first time I heard the term *alumni*. Later I learned that *alumni* meant students who had graduated.

Mr. McCloud showcased the success of alumni who once were members of the marching band. In some cases, he invited alumni to speak during band practices. In other instances, it was normal for alumni to randomly stop by to visit Mr. McCloud and encourage students. During those times, Mr. McCloud typically introduced them by telling band members when they graduated and what they did post–high school graduation. Unbeknownst to my peers and me, being exposed to successful alumni was another method our music teacher used to model his high expectations of us. I recall meeting marching band alumni from various fields including education, art and entertainment, medical science, carpentry, law, theology, political science, electrical engineering, auto mechanics, and the United States military, just to name a few.

Mr. McCloud and Me (2014)

Subconsciously, constantly being exposed to generations of successful people who once were students inspired me to aim for success so that I could one day return to inspire students. When former students visited, I observed the proud look on Mr. McCloud's face and the spark in his eyes, as if they were his own children. In those moments, I became determined to make him equally as proud after I graduated.

Mr. McCloud made it clear that he expected all his students to achieve at least a 3.0 grade point average. In addition, he made it known that students would not be allowed to participate in the band if they consistently failed academically. In order to ensure that students succeeded, he hosted study groups at the band room an hour before school began, during lunch, and up to 3 hours after school. Due to Mr. McCloud's track record for producing successful students, he was highly revered in the community and among families. Therefore, if he recommended that students come to school an hour earlier and stay later for academic assistance, parents complied. In many cases parents and legal guardians were also alumni who viewed the music teacher as a father figure. Broughton (in press) highlights the importance of educators building relationships with students and their families, just as Mr. McCloud championed.

In addition to Mr. McCloud's relationship with his students and their families, he also established strong partnerships with local businesses, which provided internships and paid work-based learning opportunities for students. Those partnerships helped fund band trips to colleges and universities and new uniforms. Local partnerships were vital because several students, including myself, could not afford to pay for these trips without additional financial support. Mr. McCloud believed in fostering independence and a strong work ethic in his students. He'd ensure that at least 50% of the trip was paid for, while he created opportunities for students to raise the remaining balance with structured fundraisers such as fruit drives, candy sales, soul food dinners, and bake sales. In retrospect, I understand that he supported his students while also ensuring that we earned everything we received. In order to ensure that students' needs were met, Mr. McCloud was one of the first persons who arrived at school daily and among the last to leave. Out of my 4 years in high school, I do not remember him being absent any more than once or twice. I do not highlight his attendance record to suggest that teachers should not take off as needed. Self-care and mental breaks are important for teachers. However, I highlight Mr. McCloud's attendance record to show the depth of his commitment to his students.

Mr. McCloud was the first adult in my life who influenced me to aim high academically. He refused to settle for less from any of his students regardless of whether they were in special education, general education courses, or the gifted and talented program. His level of expectation remained consistent for all of us. As a result of his demand for excellence, I eventually started rising to his expectation. By the time I became a sophomore, my respect for Mr. McCloud climaxed and I loved being a member of the band. Thereafter, I worked hard academically so that I would not disappoint the band director, who was also my music teacher. Before I knew it, I was a junior and finally a graduating senior. Mr. McCloud ensured that all seniors auditioned for music scholarships at several universities. To my surprise, I received full music scholarships to Benedict College, Florida Agricultural and Mechanical University, and South Carolina State University. Shortly after receiving the music scholarships, I became the first person from

Linard H. McCloud Fine Arts Center Naming Dedication (2016)

my family to graduate from high school and enter college and chose to attend Benedict College in South Carolina.

While in college, I often reflected on Mr. McCloud's expectation of alumni. He always said, "we send you to college to graduate." Therefore, in the back of my mind I always told myself, "I better do well in college because I cannot return home to Mr. McCloud without a degree." By that time, I had started to believe in myself as a young adult and engaged in self-empowering activities such as reading extensively, building relationships with progressive people, and pursuing memberships in organizations on campus such as Alpha Phi Alpha Fraternity and the gospel choir. Eventually, I became interested in furthering my education through graduate school. Upon completing my undergraduate degree in philosophy, I entered graduate school programs at Howard University and The George Washington University, earning three master's degrees consecutively, followed by a doctoral degree in educational leadership and policy studies.

It is because of the culturally responsive and effective teaching that Mr. McCloud delivered in the classroom and beyond that I went from being a special education student at a Title I school to possessing a doctoral degree. His pedagogical practices directly aligned with Ladson-Billings's (1995) culturally relevant pedagogy tenets, which include academic success, cultural competence, and critical consciousness. I encourage all preservice and inservice teachers, educational leaders, and policymakers to use Mr. Linard McCloud as a model for educating children. As a current school administrator, I frequently tell stories about Mr. McCloud to my teachers, particularly to improve our family engagement, classroom management, teaching practices, and student–teacher relationships. Similarly, as a university professor who develops future teachers and school administrators, I consistently present Mr. McCloud as a model of excellence for culturally responsive and relevant teaching.

RECOMMENDATIONS FOR TEACHER EDUCATION PRACTITIONERS

Each chapter in this volume will share similar stories about teachers whom the authors deem as effective, while concluding with practical recommendations for current and preservice teachers to employ in their practices. Likewise, I share my practical recommendations for teachers and those who are studying to become teachers based on my experience with Mr. McCloud, whom I consider to be a Dreamkeeper. I recommend that teachers employ the following practices that do not require hierarchical permission or district funding, but do require intentional planning, intrinsic motivation, and a strong work ethic:

- Be clear about your expectations and build capacity for students to meet them.
- Be fully present for your students (i.e., physically, emotionally, and mentally).
- Show students various forms of successful outcomes (e.g., alumni and mentors).
- Build relationships with families and partnerships with community stakeholders.
- Be culturally relevant and culturally responsive inside the classroom and beyond.

- Support students while also teaching them self-sufficiency and independence.
- Provide opportunities for your students beyond the classroom setting (e.g., fieldtrips, internships, and workforce development).
- Be consistent.

REFERENCES

Broughton, A. (in press). Turning up with the torch: The transformational power of a legacy of male "warm demanders." In A. L. Ellis, N. Bryan, Y. Sealey-Ruiz, I. Toldson, & C. Emdin (Eds.), *The impact of classroom practices: Teacher educators' reflections on culturally relevant teachers*. Information Age.

Bryan, N. (2020). "To me, he teaches like the child learns": Black maternal caregivers on the pedagogies and schooling practices of a Black male kindergarten teacher. *The Urban Review*. https://doi.org/10.1007/s11256-020-00577-9

Ellis, A. L., & Hartlep, N. D. (2017). Struggling in silence: A qualitative study of six African American male stutterers in educational settings. *The Journal of Educational Foundations, 30*(1/4), 33–62.

Howard, T. C. (2001). Telling their side of the story: African American students' perceptions of culturally relevant teaching. *The Urban Review, 33*(2), 131–149.

Irvine, J. J., & Fenwick, L. T. (2011). Teachers and teaching for the new millennium: The role of HBCUs. *Journal of Negro Education, 80*(3), 197–208.

Ladson-Billings, G. (1995). But that's just good teaching! The case for culturally relevant pedagogy. *Theory Into Practice, 34*(3), 159–165.

Ladson-Billings, G. (2009). *The dreamkeepers: Successful teachers of African American children*. Jossey-Bass.

Milner, H. R., IV. (2011). Culturally relevant pedagogy in a diverse urban classroom. *The Urban Review, 43*, 66–89.

Paris, D., & Alim, H. S. (Eds.). (2017). *Culturally sustaining pedagogies: Teaching and learning for justice in a changing world*. Teachers College Press.

CHAPTER 2

"Perfect Practice Makes Perfect"

Sister Mary Regis, OSP— Tempered Radical and Refined Revolutionary

Judy Alston

Being promoted from Mrs. Graham's 3rd-grade class at Cathedral School in Charleston, South Carolina, in 1974 meant that your 4th-grade teacher was going to be Sister Mary Regis. (And you could also look forward to having Sister Regis again in the 7th grade.) For most of us, we moved into that next grade with fear and trepidation that was based on facts and fiction about our new teacher. Simply put, she was *no joke*! She was a great teacher. Yet she was a serious disciplinarian (with a drawer full of paddles), but she also tempered that with love and grace. She would say to us, "While people say that practice makes perfect, I say: 'perfect practice makes perfect.'" This was a lesson that we learned time and time again during our penmanship lessons where we could only use a cartridge fountain pen with either blue or black ink. She did not believe in ballpoint pens at all. She also believed in regular-ruled loose-leaf paper, no tear-outs with frayed edges. Not to mention, we had to place our nondominant hand on the paper at a particular angle while writing with the other. That mantra "perfect practice makes perfect" has echoed throughout my life, my teaching, and my leading.

For me, Sister Mary Regis was also the embodiment of what I learned is called a "tempered radical" (Meyerson, 2001) as well as what I would eventually coin, a "refined revolutionary" (Alston, 2018). This chapter will highlight an extraordinary teacher and explore the pedagogy that she used as well as the practical life lessons that she taught, which are still solid lessons for any future teacher or educational leader in the 21st century.

OBLATE SISTERS OF PROVIDENCE

The Oblate Sisters of Providence (OSP) was founded in 1829 by Mother Mary Lange and Father James Hector Joubert in Baltimore, Maryland. They responded to the "needs of the time" and became the first successful Roman Catholic sisterhood in the world that was established by women of African descent (see website at http://oblatesisters.com). The Oblate Sisters live to "bring joy, healing and the liberating, redemptive love of the suffering Jesus to the victims of poverty, racism and injustice despite contradictions, prejudice and pain." Morrow (2002) noted that

> In forming a community of black women religious within the Roman Catholic Church, the Oblate Sisters of Providence had indemnified the virtue of black women in defiance of prevailing social attitudes . . . challenging white society's controlling images of black women and replacing them with their own self-images. (p. 141)

To this end, the Oblates have left an indelible mark on the education and edification of Black and Hispanic children for 190 years. There are so many of us who are their legacy.

SISTER MARY REGIS, OSP

My favorite OSP was born in 1920 in Yonkers, New York. Ann Cornelia Bacon later became the teacher that I knew and loved, Sister Mary Regis, OSP. In her early years, Ann and her family moved to Frederick, Maryland. Upon her death, an article in *The Baltimore Sun* (2007) stated:

> She attended elementary and high school at St. Frances Convent . . . in Baltimore. After graduating from high school in 1940, she entered the Oblate Sisters of Providence; she professed her vows in 1943. She received a bachelor's degree in elementary education from the College of Notre Dame of Maryland. Sister Mary Regis began teaching at St. Pius V Parochial School in Baltimore in 1947. Other local teaching assignments included St. Francis Xavier Parochial School and St. Cecilia Parochial School from 1963 to 1964. From 1964 to 1965, she was principal of St. Gerard Parochial School in Aiken, S.C., and later held teaching assignments in Wilson, N.C., Washington and Charleston, SC. She taught from 1979 to the middle-1980s at Holy Name of Mary Parochial School in Chicago, and her final teaching assignment was at Our Lady of the Divine Shepherd in Trenton, N.J. She retired in the early 1990s. In 1975, Fuller

& Dees Marketing Group named Sister Mary Regis "Outstanding Teacher of America." Sister Mary Regis, who had lived at her order's mother-house in Arbutus since 1997, enjoyed reading, music and watching educational TV.

The one line that really caught my eye in the article was that she was named "Outstanding Teacher in America" in 1975, which was the same year that I was in her class for the second semester of the 4th grade. We were never told this at our school.

INTENTIONALITY—THE BOTH/AND:
TEMPERED RADICAL AND REFINED REVOLUTIONARY

We live in a space and time where we are in desperate need of strong, effective, ethical, and socially just leadership more than ever. We need leaders who are interested in service and serving, first. If there's ever been a time in history for a change . . . now is that time. We need leaders who are willing to rock the boat from within and if—and when—necessary, step out of the boat to create something new. It's #TimesUp for leadership just as it has been #TimesUp for the "okey-doke."

For those of us who have been marginalized, particularly Black folk, we recognize social justice leadership as foundational in our collective epistemology and responsibility. Those of us who have been subjugated and discriminated against have not only said #TimesUp throughout history but have acted in ways that show what we do when time is up. One need only ask the spirits of Harriet Tubman, Sojourner Truth, Julia Foot, Jarena Lee, Thea Bowman, Praithia Hall, and many others who acted with strong and enduring leadership when time was up on injustices toward people of color as well as women.

As the writer of the Book of Ecclesiastes says, "there's nothing new under the sun" (*NIV Bible*, Ecclesiastes 1:9). Then a couple of chapters later in that same book, the writer goes on to note:

> For everything there is a season, and a time for every purpose under heaven: a time to be born, and a time to die; a time to plant, and a time to pluck up that which is planted; a time to kill, and a time to heal; a time to break down, and a time to build up; a time to weep, and a time to laugh; a time to mourn, and a time to dance; a time to cast away stones, and a time to gather stones together; a time to embrace, and a time to refrain from embracing; a time to seek, and a time to lose; a time to keep, and a time to cast away; a time to rend, and a time to sew; a time to keep silence, and a time to speak; a time to love, and a time to hate; a time for war, and a time for peace. (*NIV Bible*, Ecclesiastes 3:1–8)

Given that context, I ask the question using the infamous words from 1982 and the Paisley Park disciples (Morris Day & The Time), "What time is it?"

What time is it? It's time for the new. At one point, the "new" was the role of the tempered radical. Debra Meyerson (2001) stated that:

> Tempered radicals are people who want to succeed in their organizations yet want to live out their values or identities, even if they are somehow at odds with the dominant culture of their organizations. Tempered radicals want to fit in and want to retain what makes them different. They want to rock the boat and they want to stay in it." (p. xi)

Along with being a tempered radical, from my perspective, it is also time for a new boat or other means of transport. It is time for a new way of leading. It is time for a new way of being in the world. It is time for some of us to be tempered radicals, yet it is also time to step out of the boat and become refined revolutionaries. *Refined* means:

1. with impurities or unwanted elements having been removed by processing—like the "refiner's fire" (Zechariah 13:9) being constantly purified in the processing
2. elegant and cultured in appearance, manner, or taste—polished and urbane
3. developed or improved so as to be precise or subtle—fine-tuned; perfected

Revolutionary means:

1. involving or causing a complete or dramatic change; far-reaching; profound
2. rebellious; subversive
3. bold

Thus, a refined revolutionary is one who has survived the processing, become improved, heeded the call, and stepped out of the boat to lead in a bold and subversively profound manner toward a new destiny (Alston, 2018).

Being a refined revolutionary is not new, either. There have been models for this way of leadership and being throughout the annals of time. In many ways, for Black folks as a collective, we have just become complacent or comfortable in our marginalization. In some ways, it is as Malcom X said: "Ya been had! Ya been took! Ya been

Figure 2.1. Refined Revolutionary Definition

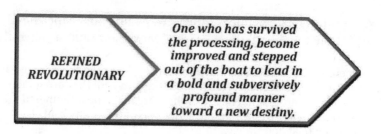

hoodwinked! Bamboozled! Led astray! Run amok!" (Lee et al., 2000).

Thus, this conceptual work on the refined revolutionary is to answer the call from our comfort zones to the learning and leading edge to be able to see the expanse of the more—the more of our dreams, the more of our purpose, the more of our lives—than just this boat that we have become so accustomed to, even while we may yet complain about it. As Pastor Courtney Clayton Jenkins (personal communication, 2017) said, "To stay in your boat when there is a call beyond is to handcuff yourself to mediocrity."

Mediocrity is simply "the way we've always done it." Mediocrity is that which can render us indifferent, unexciting, and uninspired. According to Hillman (1996) while the calling may be postponed, avoided, or intermittently missed, it may also possess you completely and eventually it will win, make its claim. Thus, leadership in this real-time 21st century must go beyond the run-of-the-mill, beyond the boat to answer the call.

It's time to step out of the boat and create new ways; lead in a new way; live in a new way. As Princess Shuri says to her brother King T'Challa in the movie *Black Panther*: "Just because something works doesn't mean that it can't be improved" (Coogler, 2018). For the refined revolutionary, it's not the thing (the boat) that may not be working, it is the me who does not work in that thing any longer. Thus it is time for transformation and moving into the new and improved—to move into a calling (a leading) that is outside of the current boat.

There is something from the past that is apropos for our walking into our destinies for life, leadership, and ultimately social justice. It is the three-pronged identities, the triumviral approach to being Alston's tempered radical/refined revolutionary (see Figure 2.2).

Figure 2.2. Tempered Radical & Refined Revolutionary Model

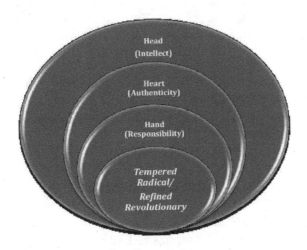

This is based on the Pestalozzian model from the 1800s. Pestalozzi (known as the Father of Modern Education) believed that education should:

> develop the powers of 'Head', 'Heart' and 'Hands'. He believed that this would help create individuals who are capable of knowing what is right and what is wrong and of acting according to this knowledge. Thus the well-being of every individual could be improved and each individual could become a responsible citizen. He believed that empowering and ennobling every individual in this way was the only way to improve society and bring peace and security to the world.(www.jhpestalozzi.org/)

This model was later adopted by Mary McLeod Bethune (a tempered radical/refined revolutionary) when at age 29 she stepped out of the boat and began Bethune-Cookman College (now university) with $1.50. Firmly committed to social justice, she became a voice of hope and optimism, inspiring pride and self-confidence in others. This three-pronged approach for Bethune's school reflected her beliefs about the role of women in society, morality, and self-reliance. She felt that women should be trained in head, hand, and heart: "their heads to think, their hands to work, and their hearts to have faith" (McCluskey, 1989, p. 122). To this end, in the song "Heads, Hearts, and Hands" dedicated to Bethune, the refrain says:

With your heads, hearts, and hands—
With hope and love—
Heads hearts and hands,
We will rise above.
Keep the faith. No matter what the world demands,
Use your heads, hearts, and hands. (Songs for Teaching, n.d.)

As I look back over my life and the early education that I received, particularly from Sister Mary Regis in 4th and 7th grade, I find this model was the foundation for how she taught and how she modeled leadership for us.

THE HEAD—INTELLECT

One thing that Sister Regis prized was intelligence. Now, that I look back at that time, I can see she emphasized all three types of intelligences —cognitive, emotional, and the character quotient (Town, 2014)—to be sure that we were equipped to move on academically and socially.

She challenged us to read everything because reading would open doors for us that we couldn't see at the time. Reading (cognitive intelligence) was a way for us to travel to places that were beyond the peninsula of Charleston and the state of South Carolina. For some students, I know that it felt like drudgery. However, I believe that she did her best to get us to understand that we could be anything that we wanted to be. As young, mostly Black children, we were more than what South Carolina history books told us we were. This was a time when we seriously celebrated Black History Week. I recall how serious she was about the Comprehensive Test of Basic Skills (CTBS) testing that we used to do. Simply put, there were basic skills that we had to know not only for our survival but also to thrive. The basics were the important foundation upon which she built us for greater.

Intelligence to Sister Regis was more than the curriculum of "reading, writing, and arithmetic." She also used emotional intelligence. She had a tough exterior, but it was clear that she cared, and as an effective leader and teacher, she established relationships with her students. This caring included how we followed directions and how we presented and comported ourselves. It was about how you wore your uniform, how you spoke, how you carried yourself.

Sister Regis also helped us develop our character as young Black children growing up in the South, and in particular in a city that wasn't that far removed from its racially divided past and still lived the reality of de facto (and some de jure) racism. About this intelligence of character, Town (2014) stated:

> Character Quotient (CQ) represents the strength of your character. While your brain may be valuable to someone else (i.e., an employer), your beliefs only hold value to you. Character Quotient raises the question of what sum you would command to compromise your beliefs. A person with a high CQ would be unlikely to compromise their beliefs based on temptations such as money or a promotion.

In respect to CQ, Sister Regis practiced and taught what Martin Luther King Jr. (1947) stated: "We must remember that intelligence is not enough. Intelligence plus character is the true goal of education." The character quotient is also embedded in the "acorn theory," offered by James Hillman (1996) in the book *The Soul's Code* and summarized as follows:

> Every acorn has within it the blueprint for a mighty and majestic oak tree. But in order for this tiny nut to reach its full potential, it needs to drop down into the dark. Into the soil. Into the muck. And then it needs to move through all of that with great effort, and burst into the light. Well, you and I are that tiny little acorn.
> Inside of us is the blueprint for a mighty oak—an amazing human with special gifts, with a unique expression, and with a special mission in this world. But we often need the muck of life, the fertilizer—the challenges, the hardships, the hurts, the setbacks, the awful upbringing—to reach our fullest potential. (https://inspirediaries.com/blueprint-for-power/)

While we may experience pain and growth in the boat as a tempered radical acorn, in order to get to our destiny as a refined radical oak tree, we will outgrow that boat. We have rooted ourselves in such a way that the boat will have to keep moving without us.

As elementary students at Cathedral School, we were the little acorns that Sister Regis and the other teachers were charged to fertilize and water so that we would grow into productive citizens. For her especially, as a Black nun, who was born at a time of legally sanctioned discrimination and hate, she wanted us to know our history and to also make history by creating a better world. We were taught by her to be tempered radicals in the boat, that is, think for yourself and learn where you are from, but not to let being in that boat limit where you would eventually go, either inside or outside of that boat. After all, she belonged to an order of nuns who themselves were founded by Mother Mary Elizabeth Lange on refined revolutionary principles —"to meet the social, religious and educational needs of poor women and children," regardless of the law of the land (McCardell, 2007).

The lessons that I learned from her still resonate in these current times of social injustice and social unrest. Those of us who live in the margins and who possess a strong mind, a strong ability to influence people on an emotional level, and a strong positive character can't get to the next personal and professional best by staying in the same boat forever. It's just like standing in an elevator and never pushing the button for the floor you want. The doors will open and close and open and close, but until you push the button to select where you want to be lifted to, nothing will happen.

THE HEART—AUTHENTICITY

Brené Brown (2010) in her book *The Gifts of Imperfection* stated that "authenticity is a collection of choices that we have to make every day. It's about the choice to show up and be real. The choice to be honest. The choice to let our true selves be seen" (p. 49). Another definition of *authenticity* noted that it is the attempt to live one's life

> according to the needs of one's inner being, rather than the demands of society or one's early conditioning. . . . The heart of leadership—this authenticity—is what moves us to use some of the most basic and important of human values—compassion, trust, empathy, forgiveness, understanding, and love—values that come from the heart. (Ryde & Sofianos, 2014)

In my own authenticity, I bring it all to the table. As Taylor (1992) stated,

> There is a certain way of being human that is my way. I am called upon to live my life in this way, and not in imitation of anyone else's. But this gives a new importance to being true to myself. If I am not, I miss the point of my life, I miss what being human is for me. . . . Being true to myself means being true to my own originality, and that is something only I can articulate and discover. In articulating it, I am also defining myself. I am realizing a potentiality that is properly my own. (pp. 28–29)

Whether inside or outside of the circle, I am called to be my true self. My identity in authentic leadership (from the heart) embodies the experiences and social factors that have shaped my beliefs. It is this connection to my soul work that causes me to behave and lead in ways that are congruent with my values, goals, and beliefs. As Polonius advised his son Laertes in Shakespeare's *Hamlet*: "This above all, to thine own self be true, and it must follow, as the night the day, thou canst not then be false to any man." Thus, stepping out of the boat may become a necessity for survival and ultimately thriving.

Sister Regis was that teacher who had an expectation that we be true to ourselves and to each other. There was no time for imitations of being anyone else. She was a frank person and said what she meant and meant what she said. Sometimes that was to a fault, but she too was human. She recognized our potential and the gifts in her students and encouraged us to hone and craft those gifts. Before I ever knew that I would be a public speaker/preacher/professor, she recognized and encouraged that gift that I didn't want to embrace. She always told me that I had a great voice. She wanted me to be true to that gift, to be authentic. During the 1977–1978 school year (7th grade), there was an Optimist International Club speech contest that we had an opportunity to compete in. Sister Regis encouraged me to write a speech for the competition, but I was too afraid to do any public speaking. For the record, I had been reluctantly doing Easter speeches at church for as far back as I could remember. I absolutely hated standing in front of an audience to talk about anything. I would get nervous and forget my lines. I told Sister Regis that I couldn't do it. She was quite disappointed in me. I did help to write the speech with another classmate who did enter and finished in third place. As I watched my classmate give the speech, I realized that I really could have done it too. While Sister Regis was disappointed, she did tell me to believe in myself. Years later and many speeches later, I remember that and am grateful. She spoke life into my heart.

THE HAND—RESPONSIBILITY

Sister Regis was also the literal "hand of responsibility" when it came to discipline. I remember so clearly taking the CTBS test one year and the instructions at bottom of the pages in each section either said "turn to the next page" or "stop, do not turn the page." One of my male classmates decided to turn the page to look ahead even though it said stop. Sister Regis had eagle eyes and saw everything. It did not go well for my classmate that day. She really did keep a draw full of paddles. I'm not suggesting that corporal punishment is right or necessary, but it was the reality that we lived. The lesson was simple: Follow directions on this simple thing so that you can create a pattern in your life of following directions because you don't know when it can save your life. Not following directions has consequences.

The hands represent an ethic of responsibility—otherwise known as "to whom much is given, much is required" (*NIV Bible*, Luke 12:48). The hands do the work, and this was a clear guiding principle of Sister Regis. Not having an ethic of responsibility with her as our teacher was not an option. Yes, we were Black and lived in Charleston in the 1970s, and while some White teachers and administrators didn't necessarily have great expectations for us or from us, she and our other Black teachers did. The truth of the matter is that we weren't really welcomed on Broad Street in downtown Charleston. Failure was not an option. Our option was to "perfectly practice" whatever the endeavor was. In other words, our option was excellence. This was the model that she lived for us.

The leadership of the hand is where one has the responsibility of knowing when to challenge the process or the status quo: Where is this boat going now? Why did we change directions? Do I need to stay in this or is it my time to get out and chart a new path? As tempered radicals and refined revolutionaries, we are called to act in deliberate and informed ways and often ways that are not in alignment with the "way we've always done it."

In leadership, we are called to action. This ethic of responsibility is as Nikki Giovanni (1988) stated: "The purpose of any leadership is to build more leadership. The purpose of being a spokesperson is to speak until the people gain a voice" (p. 135). That is who Sister Mary Regis was—a leader who helped build and edify more leaders for a time that she would never be able to see, and to be sure that we pressed toward the "unclouded lenses of [our own] potential" (Ayers, 2006, p. 7).

In this ethic of responsibility, as tempered radicals and refined revolutionaries, we must understand that we will not be rewarded by the same systems we are trying to subvert Thus it is our responsibility to make a new system—to *get out* before we go deeper into the sunken place. This is our responsibility; this is the work of our own hands.

CONCLUSION

What does this all mean in this present moment? It's time to answer the call beyond the boat. As the prophet James Brown (1970) sang, "Don't let nobody take care your business better than you do." You have to step out and lead. There can be tension in moving between tempered radical and refined revolutionary because of fear of the unknown coupled with the adrenaline to make a change and do transformative work. These two identities are not mutually exclusive. It really is all about time and knowing when to move; it is chess, not checkers.

It is then in the context as the living legacy of Sister Mary Regis that I write and speak grounded in Foucault's (2001) work on the Greek concept of *parrhesia*, which literally means "all telling," but implies not only freedom of speech, but also the obligation to speak the truth for the common good, even at personal risk. It is not only speaking the truth but walking that truth out. Walking it out may mean that you start water-walking onto your next boat. This stepping out is grounded in head, heart, and hand—intellect, authenticity, and responsibility.

Because we stand upon the shoulders of so many tempered radicals and refined revolutionaries, we need to make sure that the legacy does not crumble but is strengthened. I am the preacher, professor, leader, and person who I am today because of my experiences with Sister Mary Regis. I open my mouth when I'm teaching sometimes, and I really do hear her. I give certain looks to my students, and it is a look that I learned from her. It is certainly present when I talk with my doctoral students about APA formatting and I say, "perfect practice makes perfect."

Before Sister Mary Regis passed away in 2007, I had the opportunity to reconnect with her that year. I found her at the Oblates' motherhouse in Arbutus, Maryland. We spoke a few times on the phone and via email, and I was able to send her copies of a few of my book chapters as well as a couple of my books. She simply said to me: "Judy, I am so proud of you."

REFERENCES

Alston, J. (2018, February). *#TimesUp: Stepping out of the boat to lead. Moving from tempered radical to refined revolutionary* [Lecture]. MACH III: Building on Resilience Lecture Series at Prairie View A & M University, Prairie View, TX.

Ayers, K. (2006). *To whom much is given: The definitive guide to demystifying the doctoral experience for women.* Esperanza Communications.

The Baltimore Sun. (2007, December 15). Sister Mary Regis, 87. https://www.baltimoresun.com/news/bs-xpm-2007-12-15-0712150288-story.html

Brown, B. (2010). *The gifts of imperfection: Let go of who you think you're supposed to be and embrace who you are.* Hazelden.

Brown, J. (1970). It's a new day [Song]. King Records.

Coogler, R. (2018). *Black Panther.* Walt Disney Studios Motion Pictures.

Foucault, M. (2001) *Fearless speech.* (Pearson, J., Ed.). Semiotext(e).

Giovanni, N. (1988). *Sacred cows . . . and other edibles.* Quill/William Morrow.

Hillman, J. (1996). *The soul's code: In search of character and calling.* Random House.

King, M. L., Jr. (1947, February). The purpose of education. *The Maroon Tiger.* https://kinginstitute.stanford.edu/king-papers/documents/purpose-education

Lee, S., Worth, M., Perl, A., Blanchard, T., Washington, D., Bassett, A., Hall, A., (2000). *Malcolm X.* Warner Home Video.

McCardell, P. (2007, February 14). Mother Mary Elizabeth Lange, founder and first superior of the Oblate Sisters of Providence. *The Baltimore Sun.* https://www.baltimoresun.com/features/bal-blackhistory-lange-story.html

McCluskey, A.T. (1989). Mary McLeod Bethune and the education of black girls. *Sex Roles, 21*(1/2), 113–126. https://doi.org/10.1007/BF00289731

Meyerson, D. E. (2001). *Tempered radicals: How people use difference to inspire change at work.* Harvard Business School.

Morrow, D. B. (2002). *Persons of color and religious at the same time: The Oblate Sisters of Providence, 1828–1860.* University of North Carolina Press.

Ryde, R., & Sofianos, L. (2014). Creating authentic organizations: Bringing meaning and engagement back to work. Kogan Page.

Songs for Teaching. (n.d.). Heads, hearts, and hands. https://songsforteaching.com/blackhistorymonth/mmbethune.php

Taylor, C., (1992). *Multiculturalism and "The politics of recognition."* Princeton University Press.

Town, D. (2014, December 16). Effective leadership: The three types of intelligence you need. *Saba Blog.* https://www.saba.com/es/blog/effective-leadership-the-three-types-of-intelligence-you-need

CHAPTER 3

Undoing My Miseducation
Lessons Learned from Brother Kmt Shockley

Ramon B. Goings

In education, why do we continue to try to teach a dog how to meow like a cat?

—Brother Kmt Shockley

The opening quote came from Kmt Shockley (hereinafter referred to as Brother Kmt), a Black male Afrocentric education scholar and professor, last year during his visit to one of my graduate educational leadership courses. During his lecture he shared a tale about a dog who was put into school. When the dog first entered school, he was instantly trained to meow like a cat. At first, the dog continued to bark like a dog as that was what he was born to do. However, the longer he remained in "school," he was shown through achievement tests how barking was an inferior quality. Simultaneously, the dog was told that meowing is the best quality you can learn. At the conclusion of the dog's education career he learned how to meow, but when looking in the mirror the dog did not recognize himself as he began to take on the phenotypical qualities of a cat.

As Brother Kmt narrated this story (along with visuals of the transformation of the dog) for my students, they began to make the correlation with how the dog represented Black children in schools and how they are often taught to value and take pride in Eurocentric ideals, education, and culture (i.e., meowing) to the detriment of knowing about the greatness of African people. In addition to sharing this story, Brother Kmt also had students complete a questionnaire that tested their knowledge of European and African history. As predicted, students knew random European facts, such as "Who sailed the ocean in 1492," but were unfamiliar with African historical questions, such as "Who created the step pyramids?" During the lecture I could see that my students (majority Black) were reflecting about how they were educated to know so much about Europeans, but taught so little about Africans. In essence, many were coming to a realization about the ways their education was indeed a miseducation (Woodson, 1933/1993).

Their experience in this class brought me back to my journey to undo my own miseducation and the power that Brother Kmt, who had been my professor during my doctoral program, had had on my (re)education. Thus, in this chapter I seek to highlight the effectiveness of Brother Kmt's teaching and his impact on my life being a Black male scholar. I contend there are many lessons learned from his teaching style and approach that can inform educators who are committed to truly educating Black people.

To begin, I first provide a rationale as to why this chapter focuses on a college professor given the aims of the book focus on K–12 educators. Similar to many Black children attending U.S. public (or private) schools, I had only one Black teacher in my entire K–12 career. While that teacher had some impact on my trajectory, I do not believe I was taught from a perspective that centered my Africanness until I encountered Brother Kmt. While my experiences with Brother Kmt in this chapter have higher education as the contextual backdrop, the lessons I learned from his teaching are applicable for the K–12 setting. Furthermore, given his past experiences as a K–12 educator and administrator, I believe that Brother Kmt exuded many of the pedagogical and relational qualities that are transferrable and necessary for K–12 teachers to cultivate the genius in their Black students.

In the remaining sections of this chapter I will provide context for how Brother Kmt supported my (re)education. First, I explore my K–12 schooling and then my undergraduate educational experiences to illustrate the ways I was miseducated. Then I discuss how my doctoral classroom experiences and relationship with Brother Kmt impacted my life and trajectory as a scholar. Lastly, I provide implications and recommendations for educators who are committed to educating Black people.

HOW SCHOOLING SERVED AS THE FOUNDATION OF MY MISEDUCATION

The same educational process which inspires and stimulates the oppressor with the thought he is everything and has accomplished everything worthwhile, depresses and crushes at the same time the spark of genius in the Negro by making him feel that his race does not amount to much and never will measure up to the standards of other peoples. (Woodson, 1933/1993, p. xiii)

In many ways this excerpt from Carter G. Woodson in *The Miseducation of the Negro* summarizes my K–12 educational experience. As a child in school, I always had an internal feeling that what I was learning was not useful. I never saw myself or my experiences as a Black boy reflected in my education. For instance, when we would learn about American history, if the history of African Americans was included in the lesson it often started with Africans being slaves. As a kid I could not help but think that my ancestors started as slaves. There was never a discussion about the centuries of African brilliance that graced the earth before chattel slavery, like King Namer, Imhotep, and Mama King Hatshepsut (see Shockley, 2008, for a discussion of these brilliant Africans).

Not only did the content of the curriculum signal the inferiority of Black people, but also the physical conditions in which I was educated set a signal to me about my importance. As discussed in my prior work (Goings, 2016), in the 6th grade I attended a public school that was majority Black and Latinx where in my science class, because there were more students than desks, I had to sit on top of a laboratory table to take notes. At the time, I did not recognize the impact of this, however, in the 7th grade when my mother enrolled me in a private school (majority White), I was able to see how resources were not available in public schools to children who looked like me.

In conjunction with having a curriculum that lacked any relevance to my life and being educated in inequitable educational environments, my miseducation was grounded in not having access to educators who reflected my lived experience. To put this in perspective, my only Black teacher during my K–12 experience was my 7th-grade social studies teacher. Unfortunately, as current data suggests, Black children are likely to go their entire educational experience and not see an educator who looks like them (Goings et al., 2018).

Given the lack of access to Black male teachers during my K–12 experience, I often used television as a source of what "success" looked like. Thus as a child I wanted to be somehow involved in the music industry. Because of my ability to pick up any instrument and play, I became very interested in composing and creating music. When I would watch the videos of Michael Jackson, my favorite musician, I would ask, "Well, who created all of his music?" I would often get the response: "Quincy Jones." Thus, when I enrolled at a small liberal arts college in the South, I had the goal of majoring in music so I could learn to compose like Quincy Jones. Naively, I thought that since I was attending college I would be exposed to the rich histories of African people; however, I would quickly see how my undergraduate experience was much more of the same and would reinforce my miseducation.

THE UNDERGRADUATE EXPERIENCE: REINFORCING THE MISEDUCATION

The "educated Negroes" have the attitude of contempt toward their own people because in their own as well as in their mixed schools Negros are taught to admire the Hebrew, the Greek, the Latin, and the Teuton and to despise the African.
(Woodson, 1933/1993, p. 1)

While Woodson's (1933/1993) critique of the schooling received by "educated Negroes" was written almost 100 years ago, his words capture my undergraduate experience. As a music education major, I came into college with the idea that I would learn all of the techniques and strategies to create contemporary R&B and hip-hop music. However, my program, and many music programs across the country, were focused on giving everyone a strong foundation in classical (i.e., European) music.

Throughout my classes we learned in depth about the contributions of classical composers and musicians like Mozart, Beethoven, Bach, Stravinsky, and Brahms. While I always appreciated their contributions to music, in my mind I always thought, "Well, where are the Black composers? I know we were influencing music too!" Unfortunately, I went through my entire music education program and was introduced to only one Black composer, Scott Joplin, and this was only because I was interested in playing ragtime and found out via my own research that he was Black.

Although I excelled in college academically, at times I had an internal conflict. For instance, I often felt that in our music theory courses because we were being trained to identify and compose via classical approaches to theory that my creativity as a burgeoning R&B music producer was being stifled. Now looking back and analyzing my experience through the metaphor described by Brother Kmt at the beginning of the chapter, in many ways my program was teaching me how to "meow," when deep down I knew that I wanted to "bark." Overall, my schooling experiences ensured my miseducation was engrained. However, it was not until attending a historically Black college and university (HBCU) and meeting Brother Kmt that I would begin to undo my miseducation.

TOWARD A (RE)EDUCATION WITH BROTHER KMT

Given my K–12 and undergraduate experiences, when I made the decision to enroll in a doctoral program, I wanted an educational experience that was centered on Black people and solving issues impacting the education of Black children. As a result, I attended a mid-Atlantic HBCU to complete my doctoral degree. This choice was also made given the evidence that HBCUs create welcoming environments for Black students where they can be challenged by faculty who are truly concerned and committed to their success (Palmer et al., 2016). Throughout my time there I always felt at home and believed my professors were there to push me to be great. Additionally, this was my first experience having Black professors and reading books and articles written by Black scholars. While I did not know it at the time, enrolling in the urban educational leadership program at that university was the best educational decision I have ever made. As a new student attending my first HBCU, I was fascinated by being in an educational setting with a majority of Black students compared to my undergraduate and master's programs, where I was often the only Black male in the class.

Although I had seen "Dr. Kmt Shockley" listed as the course instructor for one of my first courses, I did not know who he was. As the class was beginning, the door opened and to my surprise a 6'4" Black man wearing a dashiki and sandals entered the classroom and set up his materials at the front of the class. From the outset, his approach to teaching was that he wanted to create the strongest Black scholars as possible and that he was going to push us in ways that would get us through the dissertation process.

Once he passed out the syllabus, my classmates and I were shocked at the number of readings for each week. As he heard us grumbling about the workload, in a somewhat sarcastic tone he said, "Well, you didn't think you were going to just get handed a doctorate, like they do the master's degree, did you? I've got to push you to write a dissertation, and in order to do so, you've got to be well read." To my surprise, our syllabus contained readings from predominantly scholars of color. We read works from Gloria Ladson-Billings, Molefi Asante, and Pedro Noguera, to name a few. For some, this approach may have been off-putting; however, it made me feel that he was concerned about our success. Additionally, being able to see a Black male at the front of the class was important to me. In some ways I felt a sense of pride that my education was in the hands of a Black professor.

One particular experience that was transformative in my academic career was receiving Brother Kmt's feedback on my first paper. Up until this point I believed I was a good writer, given my high grades in my undergraduate and master's studies. However, to my surprise on page 3 of the document it had a big circle in red that said "I stopped here. You need to see a writing coach." At the time, I was shocked at the comment and thought that he was wrong. During our conversation about the comment he explained that my writing was not ready for dissertation writing and that was what he was preparing the class to do. He suggested that I continue to read academic writing as that would help improve my writing. After getting over the disappointment of the grade, I took his advice and for the next year read one article per weekday, from various academic authors and researchers. This experience with Brother Kmt was transformational as I began to seriously study academic writers and started to develop a sense of how to write academically. I came to understand that he actually cared about my progress enough to provide me critical feedback that what I was producing was not strong enough to finish the program. Now reflecting on this experience, this was the moment where I had an "aha" moment and began to take myself seriously as a thinker and writer.

Being Introduced to Afrocentric Education

Our next class together, Philosophy of Education, would really open my eyes to how Brother Kmt was trying to cultivate our knowledge of Black people. In a typical Philosophy of Education class, you may engage in various philosophical viewpoints that are often centered on European philosophers (e.g., Aristotle, Plato, and so on). However, in this class Brother Kmt centered the course on African views and philosophy.

When first being introduced to the notion of African-centered education, I believed (because of my own miseducation) that African-centered education was a radical approach to education where Black children only learned "Black stuff." However, as I would learn in this course and through my readings about Afrocentric education, this was not the case. As described by Shockley (2011a), African-centered education is grounded in several constructs:

> Identity—the importance of identifying the Black child as an African; pan Africanism—the idea that all Black people in the world are Africans; African culture—the long-standing tradition of Blacks using African culture to sustain themselves and bring order to their lives and communities; African values adoption and transmission—inclusion of an African ethos into educational process for Black children; Black nationalism—the idea that Blacks, regardless of their specific location, constitute a nation; community control with institution building—the ability to make important decisions about the institutions that exist in one's community; and education as opposed to schooling—education is the process of imparting upon children all things they need to provide leadership within their communities and within their nation, while schooling is a training process. (p. 1032, emphasis added)

In an attempt to discredit the African-centered view, pundits have described African-centered perspectives as being a radical movement whose mission is to overthrow the American way of life. For example, Arthur Schlesinger Jr. (1998) argued that the spreading of Afrocentrism will dilute the American identity and claimed, "It is hard to see what living connection exists between American Blacks today and their heterogeneous West African ancestors three centuries ago" (p. 87). Schlesinger's argument was misguided, as the goal of an African-centered education is no different from various religious or ethnic groups who create schools, recreation centers, and human service organizations to better serve their people. For example, in cities throughout the United States parents send their children to various Catholic, Judaic, and Christian schools, which assert their religious beliefs as the center of student learning and understanding. However, these schools are never accused of being radical or revolutionary. While these groups are allowed to transfer their ideas and beliefs freely, why are Afrocentric schools and ideas scrutinized so heavily?

As someone not exposed to these ideas before this class, my mind was certainly on fire. In many ways as the beginning story suggested, I quickly realized the ways in which I was being taught in school to meow like a cat, when I should have been learning how to be a dog.

After being introduced to this notion of an African-centered education, I immediately began to replay the ways in which the education I had received until that point was indeed a Eurocentric education. Additionally, my experience in class signaled to me that I needed to do more reading and thinking to undo some of the misconceptions I had about African-centered education. My experience in this class sent me on a reading expedition to learn more. I began to read the works of Na'im Akbar (1996, 1998), Molefi Asante (1982, 1998, 2000), and Marimba Ani (1994), just to name a few. Again, important to my maturation as a scholar was that Brother Kmt was Black and truly invested in my development as a scholar and was willing to challenge my thinking.

Using Course Assignments to Engage in (Re)education

In typical doctoral classes, your assignments can involve writing a paper related to the course content. While this was an approach used by Brother Kmt, he also gave writing assignments that required us to make connections between Africans (before chattel slavery) and examine how their train of thought was still apparent in today's society. In one paper, I made the argument that Greek philosophers are often given credit for ideas when in fact those ideas were developed by Africans before them. I then gave an example from Aristotle who argued "misfortune shows those who are not friends really, but only because of some casual utility" (Aristotle, ca. 350 BCE/1935, p. 358). Aristotle argued that you are able to identify your friends in times of adversity because some friends are only around because of a benefit they receive through your friendship.

In my paper, I argued how this idea should not be given credit to Aristotle when it shows up in the works of Amenemhat I, who introduced this concept during the 12th Dynasty in Egypt (1991–1962 BCE) when he stated, "It was the one who ate my food who disdained me; it was the one whom I gave my hand that aroused fear with the kindness I showed" (Asante, 2000, p. 70). I then made the connection to how Amenemhat I's idea was articulated by Malcolm X (1965), who stated, "The thing to me worse than death was the betrayal. I could conceive death. I couldn't conceive betrayal" (p. 574). I then concluded the paper tracing this concept to rapper Notorious B.I.G. (1994), who stated, "Damn, people want to stick me for my green / and it ain't a dream things ain't always what they seem / it's the ones that smoke witcha and see ya picture / now they wanna grab the guns and come getcha."

I share details from this assignment for several reasons. First, this particular assignment allowed me to develop an appreciation for African thought. Second, this assignment showed me the ways in which European thought is often held as the "gold standard" when in fact these ideas were generated by Africans. Moreover, I greatly appreciated how the assignment was relevant to me as it allowed me to take direction in how I made the connection of African thought to modern times as I was able to bring hip-hop into my discussion in the paper. I believe one of the reasons Brother Kmt was successful is because he pushed us as Black thinkers to practice critiquing ideas and beginning the process to generate knowledge. Not only were Brother Kmt's assignments culturally responsive, as described in the next section he went out of his way to push me to finish the dissertation and consider becoming a professor.

Pushing Me to Finish the Degree and Become a Professor

As I proceeded through my doctoral program, Brother Kmt kept in contact with me on my progress. In Qualitative Research, our last class together (and my last in the program), I began to discuss an interest in becoming a college professor. Initially, I had a misconception about what college professors did, however, once I expressed my interest to Brother Kmt he began to prepare me for the realities of being a professor and homed in on the importance of my writing ability and publishing. During our initial conversations I believe he wanted to see if I was serious about engaging in the publication process. As a result, he provided me an additional first assignment, which was to read 10 peer-reviewed journal articles on my dissertation topic and develop a literature review from those 10 articles. When I came back and we discussed what I found, he had me repeat this process two more times for a total of 30 articles.

When I finally completed this task, he took the time to meet with me on the weekend to discuss my paper. I appreciated this as it showed his investment in my success not only to complete my doctoral program, but my ultimate success as a professor. During our subsequent conversations he provided insights on the professoriate. Additionally, when a classmate and I both began exploring the world of academic publishing, he provided key insights for us as we navigated the publishing process. In addition to supporting my writing, he found other ways for me to improve, such as sending students who were just starting out in the program to work with me on their writing. Considering where I started as a writer with Brother Kmt and his extremely high expectation of us as students and future scholars, I was honored that he believed in my ability to help other students. In fact, it was Brother Kmt pushing me to work with other students that eventually led to me to start my own business called the Done Dissertation Coaching Program (www.thedonedissertation.com), where I provide support to doctoral students and early career researchers who seek to complete the dissertation and become stronger academic writers.

IMPLICATIONS FOR TEACHERS

While Brother Kmt had a strong impact on my trajectory as an academician, I believe his approach to teaching through an African-centered lens and various techniques provide some poignant suggestions and recommendations for educators who seek to cultivate and enhance the scholarly pursuits of Black people (K–PhD). Below I share some of those recommendations, based on my experience with Brother Kmt, that should be implemented by educators.

As mentioned earlier in this chapter, as a Black man, having a Black male professor was extremely important to my development as a scholar. In fact, Brother Kmt was my first Black male professor during my postsecondary pursuits. His presence was critical as it gave me an image of who I could be and provided a sense of pride for me to know that Black men get PhDs and are national thought leaders. Thus it is imperative for K–12 schools and institutions of higher education not only to espouse the importance of having Black male teachers, but to use their resources to recruit and retain Black male educators throughout the pipeline.

Brother Kmt's approach to teaching and supporting students was grounded in African-centered thought. As a student I found this important to my success because I knew that the Black experience, culture, and traditions was the central focus in every class. Given my experience, Black children need access to African-centered teachers. To accomplish this task traditional teacher education programs will not suffice. As described in detail by Shockley (2011b), teachers of Black children will need to be "reattached" to Africa with reattachment being where "people of African descent are encouraged to engage in deep study of African culture, to practice aspects of those cultural ways, and to help to 'culturally advance' African groups such as the Akan or Igbo" (p. 171). Because of Brother Kmt introducing me to African-centered thought, I was able to begin my reattachment and transform my approach to teaching, leading, and researching about people of African descent. And for those adversaries of African-centered education who often claim it to be "radical" or "ineffective," I always ask, "Well, is our system and approach currently in place to educate Black people working?" I see African-centered education as a solution to truly educating Black people.

Another aspect of Brother Kmt's approach to teaching that can be impactful for Black children is for teachers to develop class assignments and activities that allow children to see the ways in which African thought has impacted every school subject. In my example in this chapter I found it impactful to be able to trace Amenemhat I's thought into the work of the Notorious B.I.G. Prior to this assignment, I had never heard of Amenemhat I and never made the connection that what Notorious B.I.G. rapped about had a theme that dated back to Africa. Through this assignment I gained an appreciation for the content I was learning, and this served as a critical moment in my academic career where I began to see myself as a knowledge producer, because I was able to read about my ancestors who were thought leaders of their time. Imagine if Black children in today's U.S. schools learned about the richness of African people in all content areas. Engaging in these types of assignments that are centered on African people would be transformative for Black children.

When considering developing assignments like Brother Kmt I believe it is important that these assignments are not arbitrarily done just because you believe your students have a connection to hip-hop (or any other contemporary phenomenon). I say this as it seems every day I read a story about teachers engaging in some assignment to explore history that, while not potentially intentional, is racist in nature. When educating Black children, you need teachers (as was the case for Brother Kmt) who take the time to learn African history first and then create assignments that allow students to think critically and make connections.

Lastly, Brother Kmt's stance as an educator was to ensure high standards and provide support and guidance along the way. I believe this approach is critically necessary for K–12 teachers, as when I visit classrooms, I often see either teachers with extremely high standards with no support or teachers with low standards and minimal support. To truly educate Black children, you need teachers who push their academic boundaries more than students believe they can go, but who do it in a way that students know they have a coach to always guide them along the way. Given the low expectations placed on Black children by society, they should be able to enter school and have access to teachers who believe in them and want to cultivate their genius.

CONCLUDING THOUGHTS

I must say that meeting Brother Kmt when I was a doctoral student was transformative to my practice as a researcher and teacher. I found confidence in knowing that if he could earn his doctorate, I could do the same as he was my first Black male college professor. However, what I believe was most impactful about his teaching approach was often our experiences outside of the formal classroom setting. Additionally, now that I am a professor, we still talk about navigating the academy, and he continues to be a support and provide critical insight on how I can succeed. While Brother Kmt had a positive impact on my trajectory, my only concern is, why did I (and Black children currently in schools) not have access to a teacher like Brother Kmt?

REFERENCES

Akbar, N. (1996). *Breaking the chains of psychological slavery.* Mind Productions and Associates.

Akbar, N. (1998). *Know thyself.* Mind Productions and Associates.

Ani, M. (1994). *Yurugu: An African-centered critique of European cultural thought and behavior.* African World Press.

Aristotle. (1935). *Athenian constitution, Eudemian ethics, virtues and vices* (H. Rackham, Trans.). Loeb Classical Library. Harvard University Press. (Original work published ca. 350 BCE)

Asante, M. K. (1982). *Afrocentricity.* African World Press.

Asante, M. K. (1998). *The Afrocentric idea* [rev. ed.]. Temple University Press.

Asante, M. K. (2000). *The Egyptian philosophers: Ancient African voices from Imhotep to Akhenaten.* African American Images.

Goings, R. B. (2016). The transformation from student to scholar through R.A.C.E. Mentoring. In M. Trotman Scott, D. Y. Ford, R. B. Goings, T. Wingfield, & M. Henfield (Eds.), *R.A.C.E. mentoring through social media: Black and Hispanic scholars share their journey in the academy* (pp. 3–11). Information Age.

Goings, R. B., Bristol, T. J., & Walker, L. J. (2018). Exploring the transition experiences of one Black male refugee pre-service teacher at a HBCU. *Journal for Multicultural Education, 12*(2), 126–143

Notorious B.I.G. (1994). Warning [Song]. On *Ready to Die. AZ Lyrics.* http://www.azlyrics.com/lyrics/notoriousbig/warning.html

Palmer, R. T., Walker, L. J., Goings, R. B., Troy C., Gipson, C. T., & Commodore, F. (Eds.). (2016). *Graduate education at historically Black colleges and universities: A student perspective*. Routledge.

Schlesinger, A. M., Jr. (1998). *The disuniting of America: Reflections on a multicultural society*. W. W. Norton.

Shockley, K. G. (2008). *The miseducation of black children*. African American Images.

Shockley, K. G. (2011a). Reaching African American students: Profile of an Afrocentric teacher. *Journal of Black Studies, 42*(7), 1027–1046.

Shockley, K. G. (2011b). A researcher "called" to "taboo" places? A burgeoning research method in African-centered education. *International Journal of Qualitative Studies in Education, 22*(2), 163–176.

Woodson, C. G. (1993). *The miseducation of the Negro*. Africa World Press. (Original work published 1933)

X, M., & Haley, A. (1965). *The autobiography of Malcolm X*. Grove Press.

CHAPTER 4

Two White Teachers Who Cultivated My Hidden Talents

The Story of an African American Male in Special Education

Shawn Anthony Robinson

In school, endurance and persistence eventually lead to survival, resulting in success, self-confidence, and achievement over the long term. Young children enter school joyfully, for the most part, and trust their teachers to excite them with new learning. I started school joyfully too, but my joy ended quickly and was replaced with anger, frustration, and failure. I was confused. Why did the teachers show me words, but not teach me how to read them? Why did they tell me it was because I wasn't trying hard enough? Why did they tell me things about those words I couldn't understand? It was like I was put into a high-stakes game, but no one told me the rules of the game, so I kept losing, especially as an African American boy in special education. A loser—that was the message I got early on, and it came through loud and clear. This chapter will briefly describe two White male educators who not only had an impact on my life, but also changed the trajectory of how I saw myself as a student. Both of them changed my life forever. The chapter begins with a short overview of my kindergarten and elementary experiences, then moves on to my high school experience, and finally, when I became a scholar. The chapter will conclude with a few recommendations for preservice and inservice training for teachers.

KINDERGARTEN AND ELEMENTARY EXPERIENCES

As early as kindergarten, I was put into the hallway when I couldn't do the "work" of being quiet and learning my letters. I was moved to a magnet school, and everyone hoped the dynamic educational experience would teach me how to learn. The fact that I had learning disabilities would simply be overcome with a strong focus on literature and writing in the magnet school. It is no surprise that this strategy didn't work, and I was referred to a public school that would provide special education services. The only students in special education were African American boys, and most of them were there because of frustration-fueled "bad" behavior. Not much direct instruction took place, and there was still no real understanding for why I was not learning to read and write. The behavior interventions used on me were intended to improve my ability to learn, but they did not improve my behavior or address ineffective instruction. I was disciplined on a recurring cycle, sent to the principal's office, sat in the hallway, and removed from class on a daily basis. It should be no surprise that as I missed instruction, even poor instruction, I fell further and further behind my classmates and further behind any reasonable grade-level expectation. Thus, I became an achievement gap statistic.

The message was clear—I had a language disability—but no one could hear the message, so nothing was done to address the problem. I was eventually diagnosed with dyslexia at the age of 18, after years in special education with teachers who had no idea what my educational needs were. I had been efficiently taught to hate everything to do with school and reading, making my relationship with education special for all the wrong reasons. Throughout the elementary grades, I would do everything possible to distract the teacher from calling on me. It terrified me to be asked to read aloud in front of my classmates. The teachers knew I couldn't read, and to this day, I do not understand what they thought would be achieved by humiliating me in front of my peers. I would wait, panicked, as the students to my right and left read, and as I saw my turn creeping closer, I would suddenly need to go to the bathroom. If that didn't work, I would dig in my nose as if I were drilling for oil until I made it bleed and then ask to go to the nurse's office.

I was becoming an expert in deflection. I still read on a 3rd- to 4th-grade level by the time I arrived in high school. I graduated from 8th grade as a special education student who was a behavior problem and who couldn't read or write. I was smart, I knew that was true, but I couldn't prove it to anyone since the only gauge teachers had was a standardized test or measures of classroom performance. I was pretty much a failure at both because I couldn't read. I felt like a deaf person being told to listen harder, or a blind person being shown an array of colors and then being tested on what colors were there.

HIGH SCHOOL EXPERIENCE

High school was an intensification of the elementary curriculum along a level of frustration from my inability to master academic skills because I couldn't read. I also engaged in disruptive classroom behavior to distract from my failings because I was angry that I couldn't access any of my skills or other forms of intelligence. My strengths were not welcome in this environment. I was creative, had a desire for knowledge, and I could see patterns between different ideas. I was also a leader at heart. These wonderful characteristics of mine went largely unnoticed, since my disruptive behavior and frustrations were so prominent. I got off to a bad start right at the beginning of my freshman year. The temperature on the first day was 80 degrees, and students were excited about seeing each other after months of summer vacation. Some students, like me, were roaming the hallways looking lost, and undoubtedly the upperclassmen could figure out who the freshmen were. I did not feel entirely lost because my peer group in middle school was there, and now we were high school guys together. Almost immediately, my freshman year was off to a rough start.

I was more concerned about socializing and directing the attention to me for reasons I thought made me look cool. My choices ended up being immature, which resulted in me getting me into trouble due to bad decisions. I fought with my peers, cursed at adults, and did not follow school rules. Internally, I was trying to mask the emotional pain of not being an acceptable student who could read and write. Externally, my behavior simply set me up for trouble. I was still searching for self-confidence and struggled academically, so I fought with peers in order to ease the pain. Reflecting back yields the realization that I was crying for help with no one listening to me, a 6'3" African American male in special education who seemed to be tough and managed to get into trouble in and out of school. In fact, trying to pinpoint exact memories from this year is difficult, but one that I remember captured the essence of my behavior. The school bell had rung, and this day I had picked a fight with the starting running back for the varsity football team. After school, I walked out the front doors talking tough guy language "Hey, you mother [bleep]—you hear me," and other inappropriate language.

While walking toward him, I grabbed my belt and put a lock on it, wrapped it around my hand, and walked up to him like the proverbial big bad wolf. Soon, I felt the hard concrete and realized I was on the ground getting punched. I got up and ran away as fast as possible. In spite of this and other similar incidents, I did not learn my lessons and found myself a regular in the dean's office. My behavior during my freshman year was moving downhill faster than an Olympic bobsled team due to my inability to read and lack of identity as a scholar.

My identity was that I was an African American male who couldn't read and caused teachers to feel apprehension around me. My inner picture of myself as a scholar and a leader was completely overwhelmed by a growing sense of shame and rage. Despite feeling hopeless, I was promoted to the next grade level and during my sophomore year received an opportunity that changed my life forever. As a sophomore, I was in regular fights in and out of class, and constantly used inappropriate language and displayed immaturity. Despite knowing right from wrong, I refused to follow instructions. In fact, my mouth constantly got me into trouble. I would frequently walk straight out of class and right into the office of the sophomore advisor chair/teacher—Mr. Carpenter.

A Teacher Reaches Out

Mr. Carpenter was a special education teacher, varsity basketball coach, and well respected throughout the school district and community. Things started to take a slight turn during my sophomore year in 1994 when Mr. Carpenter and other teachers took chances on me, similar to gambling at the craps table. The odds were not in my favor, but they were willing to make a big bet. While sitting in the chair outside the office, I observed students passing and friends were in and out of the other offices saying, "Shawn, what did you do now?" The door opened and a student walked out, followed by Mr. Carpenter, who said, "Shawn, please come in and take a seat." I sat down, and without wasting any time, he admitted his frustration. "Shawn, I am unsure I can continue helping you anymore because you are not making it easy for me," he stated.

I stared at him and didn't know how to respond. My behavior was so volatile, and Mr. Carpenter admitted that none of his classroom and extracurricular interventions seemed to work with me. "We need to find something that you can channel your inner anger into. I think it will be a good opportunity for you to serve as a peer mentor/coach for the adapted physical education class in the Educable Mentally Retarded program and Special Olympics (SO)," he said, as if it were a normal thing to say to me. "Me, a peer mentor," I thought to myself, and my response was, "I am not working with those [bleep]!"

Fostering My Hidden Talents as a Leader

In all honesty, the exact reasons I started working with the students in the program, and what changed my mind from that first reaction, I no longer remember. What I do remember is that from the very beginning of our time and work together, Mr. Carpenter saw my potential, and the student athletes saw me as a leader. Competitions allowed me to witness the student athletes shining and taking chances without fear. They smiled, laughed, and showed respect for each other, and I found that the student athletes I coached considered me a friend. They showed me a lot of love. My experiences of having challenges and knowing what it was like to not be seen for my strengths allowed me to feel right at home and be loved by the students.

I quickly became a valuable member in this community and learned many life lessons from the student athletes while participating as a peer mentor and coach. At that time, I did not actually know my strengths, but Mr. Carpenter's decision to get me involved in SO as a peer mentor during my sophomore year transformed my life and helped me understand my leadership abilities. His gamble paid off. I have always been athletic, so I connected immediately with the student athletes in the program. Despite not having learned to control my anger in most aspects of my life, I was able to do so when coaching SO. As a coach, besides learning the art of patience, I had to follow the SO motto to "teach the skills and spirit that define a true athlete" and "help athletes with intellectual disabilities find their own strengths and abilities" (https://www.specialolympics.org/get-involved/coach).

I Was Becoming a Leader

It was my job to give athletes the chance to reach their potential on and off the field, similar to the way Mr. Carpenter treated me. Mr. Carpenter modeled a version of leadership for me as well as provided me an opportunity to shine, which allowed me a chance to recognize and nurture other innate abilities such as trust and respect, which

Mr. Carpenter and Me (1995–1996)

boosted my self-confidence. He discovered all these other qualities despite my learning disability. I now realize that Mr. Carpenter had unlocked my potential and achievement for individual progress. This allowed me to believe I could perform at remarkably high levels when provided the right opportunities. Mr. Carpenter did not stop at seeing "the African American boy with the behavior problem." Instead, he pushed past that first impression and saw Shawn, the teenage boy, with leadership potential.

Some of the greatest experiences in my life involved coaching and helping in the classes. During the day, I was a lost and angry adolescent. On Thursday evenings, however, this same person was coaching track and field. A typical Thursday night consisted of athletes, coaches, parents, and volunteers meeting at the gym and sharing laughs, smiles, hugs, and workouts from 6–8 p.m., followed by all of us going to a local burger shop for a late dinner. On one particular Thursday night, I was asked to lead the group warm-ups. It was a privilege to ask everyone to move into a full circle and lead the warm-up exercises. After the warm-ups, we broke into groups where everyone rotated between the 50-yard dash, ball toss, and assistant walker race. At these stations, I was able to use my athletic ability to inspire the students to push themselves. Even such simple moments of successful leadership deepened my sense of purpose.

One of my vivid memories is of Danny, who lined up and turned toward me, saying, "Robinson, you are going down!" He pointed his finger at me with a smile. The starter at the finish line raised his hands and said, "On your mark, set, go!" Danny took off, and I stood for a second and then caught up to him, screaming, "Come on, come on, let's go." At the finish line, he turned to hug me and said, "Thank you." Then we walked back, and he said, "Robinson, I want you again." We lined up and the starter dropped his hand and we were off. This time Danny broke his 50-yard dash time and set a record. The smile on his face was similar to Wayne Gretzky's reaction when he set a National Hockey League record in 1994. Throughout my time at SO, I rotated to different stations where I cheered and encouraged the student athletes to push through regardless of adversity.

My role as a coach allowed me to be reliable and consistent with my responsibilities because of my love for what I was doing. Throughout my high school experience, Mr. Carpenter provided opportunities for me to shine outside of my actual classes because he obviously saw something in me that other teachers did not. As my high school career came to an end in 1996, I felt similar to Brett Favre, who won the National Football League Most Valuable Player Award in 1996. I began to see myself as valuable and received the following accolades: Volunteer Service Award; Educable Mentally Handicapped (EMH) Student Helper; Certificate of Achievement–Special Olympics; Tri-Ship Scholarship; Youth Volunteer Service Award; and Village Board of Trustees and Citizen of the Year. Throughout high school, my teachers trudged along, keeping me on the same Individual Education Program (IEP) that had been started for me in elementary school, focusing on behavior issues and not my learning disabilities from dyslexia. Their inability to recognize my true academic disability prevented each one of them from teaching me to read with an appropriate approach for students with dyslexia, and therefore I was not provided with an effective academic education until college.

Figure 4.1. Doctor Dyslexia Dude

Note. From *Doctor Dyslexia Dude* (p.26), by S. A. Robinson, I. V. Robinson, & B. Hadnot, 2018, Ripon Printers. Used with permisson.

WHEN I BECAME A SCHOLAR!

My mother was determined that I would go to college, despite the fact that I was receiving little specific instruction and therefore making minimal academic progress (Myers-Glower, 2019). She relentlessly sought out college programs for students with learning disabilities and heard about Project Success at the University of Wisconsin–Oshkosh. She took me to meet with Dr. Nash, founder and former director of the program. I was screaming, "I am a failure, I will never make it in college, I want to go home!" My steadfast mother continued to insist that I meet Dr. Nash. Once in his office, he conducted a sequence of standardized tests, beginning by asking me to read high-frequency words from an elementary grade–level list. There I sat, a high school student who could see the words but could not read or spell most of them. I stared at the paper without much expression, growing increasingly embarrassed, and becoming frustrated (see Figure 4.1).

Mr. Carpenter and Me at my PhD Commencement

Dr. Nash stopped testing and confirmed that my frustration was normal, which felt refreshing. He then said, "Shawn, I would like you to spell the word *came*," and I replied "K-A-M," and Dr. Nash said, "You have dyslexia." Dr. Nash finished and called my mother back into his office and said, "Shawn has dyslexia, and I'm accepting him into the Project Success program." This gave my mother the hope she had been seeking. I was accepted into the program after an hour-long meeting. He went on to explain, "This doesn't guarantee he will be accepted into the university, but if I accept him into the Project Success program, it is highly likely he will be accepted in the university." The entire drive home I was screaming, "I am going to college!" My narrative had changed!

In Project Success, I received explicit, sequential instruction specifically to teach me to read. I needed this targeted approach because I was a student with dyslexia. I was finally being taught how to process the sounds of the English language. I learned to read and spell basic words based on phonics and orthography, and I started to read more and more (Robinson, 2013). I was challenged with interesting concepts and higher-level thinking while at the same time I was learning the sound–symbol structure and rules of English (Wolf, 2007). While I was learning cognitively at the level of other college students, I was working my way through elementary levels of reading. By the time I was 20, my reading level had improved to that of an 8th-grader, and I was still learning. I was learning to utilize more varied instructional techniques, make connections across multiple texts and course content, and advance my overall knowledge base. I was doing all this because I was becoming a reader. I graduated with a BA and went on to earn a master's and a doctoral degree.

RECOMMENDATIONS FOR PRESERVICE AND INSERVICE TEACHERS

Based on my academic experiences and encounters with Mr. Carpenter and Dr. Nash, I believe it is necessary for teachers to assist all students who receive special education services, but especially African American boys, who routinely do not have access to transformative academic and social opportunities (Ferri, 2006; McDonald et al., 2007; Orellana et al., 2011; Robinson, 2016, 2018). Therefore, teachers may want to consider the following practices:

1. Establish early identification criteria for diagnosing a learning disability.
2. Offer effective curriculum based on the science of reading.
3. Differentiate instruction to build success and confidence.
4. Provide extracurricular opportunities for students to shine.
5. Teach safe emotional language and use it consistently when addressing disruptive behaviors.
6. Identify supports within schools and in the community.
7. Identify peers that can be role models, or help to foster the role of being a role model.
8. Recognize ways to build self-esteem and self-concept, while strengthening self-identity.

Too often, students with undiagnosed learning disabilities, particularly African American boys, are simply given more structure and standards rather than provided an adapted curriculum and appropriate instruction. As soon as these students act out of their frustration, they are seen as behavior problems (Connor, 2006). With African

American boys, this is often coupled with being seen only through their racial identity (Blanchett, 2010). Now, they are students with behavior problems. To counter the imbalances in racial identity, teachers could design academic programs to create a sense of "family" among students from linguistic and ethnic backgrounds that may be beneficial for those in special education identified as "marginalized," as the teacher may then be able to help them foster "kinship ties," which builds identity (Yosso, 2005).

CONCLUSION

Reflecting on my years of education, two strong themes stand out for me. The obvious theme is that of being an undiagnosed student with dyslexia who was consequently denied explicit, systematic language instruction. My learning needs were not met on even a basic level, and I was instead identified as an African American male with behavior problems. Each educator who was able to see beyond the behaviors and understand who I was and what I needed was White. These two teachers did not settle for me being merely another statistical expectation of failure because of my behavior and/or lack of perceived academic abilities. Furthermore, these two teachers did see my race.

However, they saw my potential of what I could become and provided me the right resources I needed. I was allowed the chance to be a leader with the Special Olympics. I became part of a community of people helping each other, keeping in mind that every individual in the Special Olympics had a gift to offer others. This was the first time I was seen as an individual with gifts and welcomed into a circle of striving people. In college, I became a reader in Dr. Nash's Project Success program. The world of language and learning opened for me after 12 years of being blocked at every turn. I entered my adult years, recapitulating a full childhood of learning that I had been prevented from enjoying. That level of learning as an adult was only possible because of the genuine skill and talent of a single brilliant White man, who saw my dyslexia as a hinderance that could be removed. Leading and reading have become the great themes of my life because of two inspiring educators who knew the value of belief and trust. Their gift to me has become my gift to others. To read is to lead.

REFERENCES

Blanchett, W. J. (2010). Telling it like it is: The role of race, class, & culture in the perpetuation of learning disabilities as a privileged category for the White middle class. *Disability Studies Quarterly, 30*(2). http://dx.doi.org/10.18061/dsq.v30i2.1233

Connor, D. (2006). Michael's story: "I get into so much trouble just by walking": Narrative knowing and life at the intersections of learning disability, race, and class. *Equity & Excellence in Education, 39,* 154–165.

Ferri, B. A. (2006). Voices in the struggle: In response to "Reigning in special education." *Disability Studies Quarterly, 26*(2), 10–14.

Hadnot, B. (2018). Doctor Dyslexia Dude [Graphic Illustrator]. Available from https://drdyslexiadude.com

McDonald, K., Keys, E., & Balcazar, C. (2007). Disability, race/ethnicity and gender: Themes of cultural oppression, acts of individual resistance. *American Journal of Community Psychology, 39,* 145–161.

Myers-Glower, M. (2019). A star is born. In S. A. Robinson (Ed.), *Narratives from mothers of children with dyslexia: Our stories for educators* (pp. 117–121). Peter Lang.

Orellana, M., Reynolds, J., & Martinez, D. (2011). Cultural modeling: Building on cultural strengths as an alternative to remedial reading approaches. In A. F. McGill-Franzen & R. L. Allington (Eds.), *Handbook of reading disability research* (pp. 219–232). Routledge.

Robinson, S. A. (2013). Educating Black males with dyslexia. *Interdisciplinary Journal of Teaching and Learning, 3*(3), 159–174.

Robinson, S. A. (2016). Supporting twice exceptional African American students: Implications for classroom teaching. *Wisconsin English Journal, 58*(2).

Robinson, S. A. (2018). Introduction: Voiceless no more. In S. A. Robinson (Ed.), *Untold narratives: African Americans who received special education services and succeeded beyond expectations* (pp. xi–xix). Information Age.

Robinson, S. A., Robinson, I. V., & Hadnot, B. (2018). *Doctor Dyslexia Dude.* Ripon Printers.

Wolf, M. (2007). *Proust and the squid: The story and science of the reading brain.* Harper Collins.

Yosso, T. J. (2005). Whose culture has capital? A critical race theory discussion of community cultural wealth. *Race Ethnicity and Education, 8*(1), 69–91.

CHAPTER 5

Married to Education

The Impact of Teacher Expectations on African American Student Success

Roslyn Clark Artis

West Virginia is among the least diverse states in America. At present, the state's Black population is 3.65%, with individuals designated as mixed-race comprising a mere 1.76% (U.S. Census Bureau, 2020). West Virginia ranks 48th of the 50 states for diversity, ahead of only Vermont and Maine in its homogeneity. These diversity numbers have remained largely unchanged since my days in primary and secondary school. According to the 1980 census, Blacks made up a mere 3.3% of the state's population (U.S. Census Bureau, 1980, p. 20). Thus, from a demographic standpoint, the more things change, the more they stay the same in the "Mountain State."

My father was a coal miner—I am, therefore, a literal "coal miner's daughter." In short, I grew up in a low-wealth, working-class family in a small Black neighborhood that existed within the context of an overwhelmingly White Appalachian state. To complicate matters, my mother is White, thereby conferring upon my brother and me, the unenviable designation of "mixed." While being of mixed race is on trend today, in the 1970s and 1980s this demographic blend resulted in merciless teasing and labels that included "zebra" and "Oreo." To make matters worse, my mother was disowned by her own family and ostracized by the Black mothers in the neighborhood for having the audacity to marry a Black man. Thus she had no resources, social support, or even basic knowledge about the complexities of managing my unwieldy hair. In sum, despite being academically strong, I grew up poor and funny looking, with low self-esteem and an overwhelming sense that I simply did not belong.

I had a clear understanding of the obvious economic and social disadvantages that came with being Black in rural West Virginia. However, by virtue of my mixed-race household, I never enjoyed the communal solidarity within the race that brought comfort and a sense of Black pride. Black history was not conversation over the dinner table. Moreover, I certainly never experienced the benefits of White privilege that should have naturally accrued to my mother, as she surrendered that advantage immediately upon her identification as a "nigger lover." In short, I was caught between the racial "rock and a hard place," struggling to find my place in the world that, at the time, did not include the "other" box on most forms. You were either Black or White—there was no in-between.

I arrived at Stratton Junior High School in 1982. Prior to that point, I'd only ever had one 1 Black teacher—Mrs. Evelyn Moore (5th grade). Moreover, I'd certainly never been in a classroom with more than a handful of Black students. However, Stratton was different—it was the Black junior high school. I had begged my parents to let me attend Stratton, which was within walking distance, rather than be bused to the predominately White, Park Junior High School. I was thrilled when they agreed.

Unfortunately, I had yet to master my unruly hair, could not afford "cool clothes," and had little experience interacting with other Black children. Thus the transition to "the Black school" was more difficult than I'd imagined in my 12-year-old mind. My sole asset was my academic ability, which quickly distinguished me from my peers. I had experienced a high level of academic success to that point and fully expected that trend to continue into junior high school. To my surprise, I would encounter Black educators who were uncompromising and equally unwilling to allow my perceived challenges to limit my own academic ability or social/emotional development even if it meant allowing me to fail in order to teach me.

JOHN AND LORRAINE SEAY

Upon arriving at Stratton Junior High School, I was assigned a schedule that would include courses taught by two African American educators who would have a profound impact on my educational and social development. Seventh-grade Physical Education was taught by Lorraine Seay, and Honors Math was taught by John Seay. The two were not only married to one another, they were in a metaphorical marriage relationship with education. I am fortunate to be among the offspring of the second union.

John and Lorraine Seay were both raised in the segregated coal fields of southern West Virginia. They attended segregated primary and secondary schools, including Stratton High School, which operated until 1967, when its students were integrated into the all-White, Woodrow Wilson High School. The building would become Stratton Junior High School, where I would ultimately encounter the Seays as a student in the 1980s. The two had a natural affinity for one another: Both aspiring educators with a love of the arts—piano, dance, and theater. The pair attended Bluefield State College, a historically Black college located in Bluefield, West Virginia.

They were outgoing and engaged fully in the social and cultural historically Black college experience. Beautiful and smart, Lorraine would pledge Delta Sigma Theta sorority and become a campus queen. The always dapper John would pledge Kappa Alpha Psi fraternity. Upon graduation, the handsome pair wed and mutually embarked on teaching careers. They occupied positions of high regard in the community as active members of their church and various civic organizations. They lived in a modest brick home less than 200 yards from their home church, Central Baptist Church, to the west and their workplace, Stratton Junior High School, to the east. In short, their world and that of the two children they would raise together, existed within scarcely more than a few square miles. Each morning, the pair would walk hand in hand to work at Stratton Junior High School, providing a striking visual image to their students of two loving marriages—a marriage between John and Lorraine, and the marriage between the couple and their calling to teach.

THE INFLUENCE OF LORRAINE SEAY

I received my first and only failing grade (ever) from Lorraine Seay. She was small in stature, with gentle features that belied her steely resolve. She walked briskly and took her work seriously. She was a coach, a mentor, a wife, and a mother. Most of all, Lorraine King Seay was no-nonsense. Physical Education was not to be taken lightly as your physiological well-being made way for intellectual agility. She believed deeply in both.

In truth, I was not opposed to the physical demands of Lorraine Seay's class, and I rather enjoyed her lively lessons on nutrition, the human body systems, and the negative impact of carcinogens. She was an excellent teacher, with an ability to balance rigor with what we now refer to as "active learning strategies." The challenge for me was the locker room. Gym in those days required you to change into your gym clothes in the presence of others and to shower and redress at the conclusion of the class. Privacy was unheard of. As a socially awkward, and woefully underdeveloped, pre-teen, I dreaded the locker room, where I was often subjected to merciless teasing about the obvious absence of anything resembling breasts and whatever other odd characteristic might capture the attention of my tormentors.

In order to avoid the unpleasant experience, I lied. I made up one excuse after another to get out of dressing for gym: I forgot my gym clothes; I have a headache; I have cramps . . . you name it, I tried it. Mrs. Seay dismissed my attestations and assigned various activities to keep me busy as I sat on the sidelines watching my classmates run laps, play sports, or engage in other coordinated physical activity. I was satisfied that I had saved myself from unnecessary anguish and diligently completed my written work.

At the conclusion of the semester, when grades were distributed, I was stunned to have earned an F in Physical Education. I appealed to Mrs. Seay to re-evaluate the grade. She patiently and systematically walked me through her grade book and the string of zeros I had accumulated—one for each day that I declined to participate. It was indisputable—I had *earned* an F. I was devastated and angry. I resorted to a strategy that most 12-year-old children employ when something they desire does not come to fruition—I begged and I cried.

In response to my futile pleas, Lorraine Seay quietly, firmly, and unapologetically taught me the most important lesson of my life: There are no excuses—if you do not perform, you will fail. You must learn to stand in the face of adversity, in whatever form it takes. Your income level, race, family circumstance, or 7th-grade bullies must never be used as reasons to not do your best. Lorraine Seay taught me resilience, and she taught me that there are consequences for the choices we make.

Mrs. Seay was not unsympathetic or unkind. To the contrary, she cared deeply for me and other students of color under her tutelage. She understood that as students of color, many of whom hailed from challenging family circumstances, we would have to develop thick skin, stiff spines, and a strong will to win. While devastating for a student who had never made even a B in school, Lorraine Seay need- ed to teach me a lesson before the stakes were too high. After all, perspective colleges would never see my 7th-grade report card. Had I not learned that valuable lesson early in my educational career, the consequences would have been far higher for me. Suffice it to say, I heard her loud and clear. It was my first and last F.

To be sure, I learned the rules of basketball, volleyball, dodgeball, and badminton in 7th-grade Physical Education, albeit from a book from my perch in the bleachers. I also learned the circulatory system, the nervous system, and the musculoskeletal system in her class. She was an excellent teacher who took pride in her craft. More impor- tantly, I learned life lessons that have been among the most valuable takeaways from my junior high school years. That is the true measure of a teacher.

THE INFLUENCE OF JOHN SEAY

Despite a strong overall academic record, I—along with countless young women of all races—experienced academic discrimination. The time-honored stereotypes resulted in generations of young women failing to explore STEM disciplines due to the perception that girls are not inherently strong in math and science disciplines. Fortunate- ly, such narrow views were not held by John Seay. To the contrary, his expectation was that every student, including young women, em- braced numeracy and mastered mathematical concepts with precision and accuracy.

I both respected and feared John Seay. He walked with his back as straight as an arrow and wielded a yard stick with authority. Mr. Seay was always impeccably dressed and had an authoritative dispo- sition. While I was too young to recognize it as such, John Seay uti- lized the Socratic method of teaching, a pedagogical strategy primarily employed in law schools. He would gaze across the sea of pupils faces until he spotted the student who appeared most uncomfortable and desirous of anonymity. That student was called on to respond to a query or, worse, solve a problem on the board in front of the class. He would walk over and stand directly over the student, yardstick tap- ping loudly on the desk, and pepper his victim with increasingly more difficult questions. "I don't know" was the worst possible answer and entirely unacceptable. Like a bug under a mean kid's magnifying glass on a sunny day, the heat of his gaze and those of your classmates was searing as you endured rapid-fire questioning that stretched your intellectual abilities and forced you to understand and articulate that which you'd mistakenly believed you did not know.

Conversely, responding correctly on the first try often resulted in a barrage of increasingly more complex problems being hurled at you. John Seay believed it was his responsibility to push you to, and well beyond, your mathematical capability. If you struggled, you were pushed harder. If you excelled, you were pushed even harder than that. While I would not suggest that the experience was pleasant, what I can say with certainty, is that I, and many other students, expanded our analytical capabilities under the watchful eye of John Seay.

While the subject matter was mathematics, Mr. Seay forced us to explain our answers under tremendous pressure. He understood that the ability to communicate, to debate, and defend your calculations and/or point of view was as critical as the underlying subject matter. As a result, his math students also became confident communicators. His speech was precise, and his grammar and diction were nothing short of perfect. Correct grammar seemed to be as important as the right answer in Mr. Seay's class. A decade later as I prepared for a moot court competition in law school, I silently thanked John Seay for planting the seeds of diction, dialog, and debate in my 7th-grade math class.

If Mr. Seay had preconceived notions about your ability or lack thereof, it was not apparent. He had no favorites. There were no teacher's pets. Everyone—boy or girl, Black or White, rich or poor—learned math in John's Seay's class. He managed his class in a disciplined way and math was the priority. He did not seek to befriend his students, only to educate them. Failure was not an option, and mastery the only expectation beyond good behavior.

I would not characterize Mr. Seay as particularly warm or paternal. Rather, he was straightforward and matter-of-fact. He had a quick wit and a dry sense of humor that I daresay eluded many of my classmates. He was an excellent teacher, who chose to teach a population of students that few expected to succeed. He seemed oblivious to that fact and taught as though he were assigned to a senior seminar class at Harvard. In short, he presumed we could do it and, through his masterful teaching style, succeeded in convincing each of us that his presumption was correct. He believed we were brilliant and developed in each student a greater sense of self-efficacy. I respected John Seay; I feared John Seay; and I am forever grateful that I was taught mathematics, among other things, by John Seay.

TEACHER EXPECTATIONS

Researchers have documented statistically significant racial differences in teachers' perceptions of students' academic skills and abilities. Equally well documented are the racial achievement gaps that persist in the American education system. These gaps have been attributed to differences in socioeconomic status, school readiness, and parent educational attainment (Ellis, 2019; Harris, 2011; Harris & Robinson, 2007). Among the practices found to positively impact the achievement gap are school climate, teacher expectations, and instructional methods (Brown, 2002).

Many studies have focused on factors associated with lack of preparation and poor performance among minority youth. Others have documented achievement gaps even among high-achieving minority students (Ford, 1998; Ford et al., 2008). In both contexts, researchers acknowledge the centrality of the teacher–student relationship to the understanding of student achievement. Specifically, the influence that teacher perception and expectations have on student academic performance are critical considerations. It stands to reason, therefore, that high teacher expectations have a strong positive impact on student self-efficacy and, ultimately, on student achievement for minority students. Similarly, low expectations often enable negative student behaviors, habits, and outcomes.

The stark differences between America's teaching workforce and the diverse student populations they serve is an unfortunate reality. Efforts are ongoing to recruit, train, develop, and deploy Black and Brown teachers, particularly in the most diverse school districts. Minority teachers like John and Lorraine Seay substantiate the importance of a diverse teaching workforce by encouraging academic excellence among minority youth as an instrument of social uplift. Clearly, many racial stereotypes held by educators are the result of negative perceptions of Black and Brown student intellectual capacity and cognitive ability (Ford et al., 2008).

Since the late 1960s, researchers have acknowledged that teacher perceptions can impact student learning and social development because such perceptions often directly influence the nature and quality of teacher–student interaction (Rosenthal & Jacobson, 1968). The Rosenthal and Jacobson study was the first comprehensive study to suggest that teacher expectations, even when based on erroneous information or assumptions, can influence the academic performance of children. This harmful practice came to be referred to as the Pygmalion Effect.

In recent years, researchers explored the subtleties and the power of these self-fulfilling prophesies on student performance. Today, researchers generally agree that teacher expectancy effects exist (Jussim et al., 2009; Wang et al., 2018). These expectations can affect child development from the first school days onward, as well as affecting later educational achievements and eventual outcomes.

Studies have shown that inaccuracy in teacher expectations is not random. Rather, perceptions of student ability tend to appear in a systematic way for different groups of students. Most notably, negative bias in teacher expectations has been found for students from socially disadvantaged families (e.g., Timmermans et al., 2016) and for ethnic minority students (e.g., Holder & Kessels, 2017). Teacher expectancy effects based on systemic biases have the potential to contribute to and exacerbate educational inequality.

Moreover, the intersectionality of teacher expectations and teacher perceptions of student ability can influence the quality of teacher instruction as well as student academic potential, emotional stability, social interactions, interest, and motivation (Farkas et al., 1990). Not surprisingly, teacher perception is a much stronger predictor of low-wealth Black student perceptions of their own academic ability as these students often have limited access to positive role models and thus lack consistent positive reinforcement of their academic abilities.

Although research aimed at understanding racial differences in teacher perceptions is ongoing, many education scholars agree that these differences are related to the assumption or stereotype that Black and Brown students are academically and socially inferior to their White counterparts.

Importantly, scholarship on race-based educational inequality has largely focused on academically underprepared and lower-performing minority students. However, racial achievement gaps also exist among high-performing students of color. High-achieving minority students are more likely to be underestimated by teachers. This performance perception mismatch has implications for the academic growth and success of high-achieving minority students. Diminished teacher expectations for high-performing students often discourage students from performing to their full potential. Undoubtedly, high-achieving minority students benefit from having teachers who motivate them to excel.

This was certainly my lived experience. The Seays—particularly John Seay—maintained exceedingly high expectations for all students and routinely heightened that standard when it became apparent that a student had greater capacity, thereby forcing that student to "level up."

LESSONS LEARNED AND IMPLICATIONS FOR PRACTICE

Negative teacher biases can function like self-fulfilling prophecies that directly affect student success. Moreover, we know that teacher expectations differ by racial groups in ways that put Black students at a disadvantage, thereby exacerbating racial achievement gaps. To the contrary, the positive perceptions of student capacity for both low- and high-achieving students can have a significant positive impact on the quality of student–teacher interactions and the resulting student achievement. Students who are encouraged and supported in their learning often excel over their less fortunate peers.

It has been said that children don't care what you know until they know that you care. While the author is unknown, the power of the statement is undisputed. "Care" can be shown in many ways. John and Lorraine Seay would not be characterized as outwardly warm, or particularly nurturing to their students. They were firm and, arguably, aloof. However, their genuine care and concern for their students was demonstrated by the example they set as high-achieving African Americans and, more importantly, their keen understanding of, and willingness to, push us beyond our perceived potential. While it was not clear to me until much later, they followed the road less traveled—they believed in us enough to push, and, when necessary, punish us. Not surprisingly, the true value of these lessons is often realized in retrospect.

Establishing and maintaining high expectations for student learning and behavior can lead to strong, positive outcomes for minority students. Beyond a large-scale diversification of the teacher workforce, which is a highly improbable short-term solution, teacher training and development presents an opportunity.

All teachers must critically examine and work to actively overcome biases that impact perceptions of student capability and performance expectations. Research-based staff development to support the fine-tuning of assessment skills and active dismantling of stereotypes is key. Self-reflection and hindsight evaluations of student performance against initial assessments may prove beneficial and assist teachers who genuinely desire to shed any unconscious bias developed as a result of their upbringing, exposure, or lived experience.

Additionally, in recent years, we have seen the emergence of a heightened sensitivity to political correctness and an outcry for the provision of safe spaces. Without question, students should be actively protected from emotional, social, or physical danger in schools. Most assuredly, psychological harm must never be inflicted at the hands of a teacher, intentionally or otherwise. However, accurate assessment of student learning and high expectations for student accountability do not equate to harm. Academic and/or grading standards should not be relaxed in order to avoid hurting a student's feelings, or worse, their ego. Accountability is caring. Loving but firm constructive correction can be a very effective strategy in motivating student achievement. Failure is not fatal—it can be instructive.

Everything I needed to know in life, I learned from a teacher—the ability to communicate effectively, calculate complex equations, think critically, and, most importantly, recognize that I am ultimately responsible for my own success. John and Lorraine Seay not only built my intellectual capacity through their carefully curated lesson plans, they also taught me confidence, character, and commitment to, and responsibility for, my own achievement. I am proud and grateful to have been among the thousands of proverbial offspring of this metaphorical marriage to education.

REFERENCES

Brown, K. E. (2002). The influence of school climate, teacher expectations, and instructional methods on student achievement of low SES African American elementary students: A case study. *Dissertation Abstracts International, 63*(07B), 3512.

Ellis, A. L. (2019). Foreword: Leveraging empirical research: Storytelling among Black educational leaders. In R. T. Palmer, M. O. Cadet, K. Le-Niles, & J. L. Hughes (Eds.), *Personal narratives of Black educational leaders: Pathways to academic success* (pp. vii–x). Routledge.

Farkas, G., Grobe, R. P., Sheehan, D., & Shuan, Y. (1990). Cultural resources and school success: Gender, ethnicity, and poverty groups within an urban school district. *American Sociological Review, 55,* 127–142. https://doi.org/10.2307/2095708

Ford, D. Y. (1998). The underrepresentation of minority students in gifted education: Problems and promises in recruitment and retention. *The Journal of Special Education, 32*(1), 4–14. https://doi.org/10.1177/002246699803200102

Ford, D. Y., Grantham, T. C., & Whiting, G. (2008). Culturally and linguistically diverse students in gifted education: Recruitment and retention issues. *Exceptional Children, 74*(3), 289–306. https://doi.org/10.1177%2F001440290807400302

Harris, A. L. (2011). *Kids don't want to fail: Oppositional culture and Black students' academic achievement.* Harvard University Press

Harris, A. L, & Robinson, K. (2007). Schooling behaviors or prior skills? A cautionary tale of omitted variable bias within oppositional culture theory. *Sociology of Education, 80*(2), 139–157. https://doi.org/10.1177%2F003804070708000203

Holder, K., & Kessels, U. (2017). Gender and ethnic stereotypes in student teachers' judgments: A new look from a shifting standards perspective. *Social Psychology of Education: An International Journal, 20*(3), 471–490. https://doi.org/10.1007/s11218-017-9384-z

Jussim, L., Cain, T., Crawford, J., Harber, K., & Cohen, F. (2009). The unbearable accuracy of stereotypes. In T. Nelson (Ed.), *The handbook of prejudice, stereotyping, and discrimination* (pp. 199–227). Psychological Press.

Rosenthal, R., & Jacobson, L. (1968). Pygmalion in the classroom. *The Urban Review, 3,* 16–20. https://psycnet.apa.org/doi/10.1037/0022-3514.69.5.797

Timmermans, A. C., De Boer, H., & Van der Werf, M. P. C. (2016). An investigation of the relationship between teachers' expectations and teachers' perceptions of student attributes. *Social Psychology of Education, 19,* 217–240. doi:10.1007/s11218-015-9326-6

U.S. Census Bureau. (1980). *Census of the Population of West Virginia.* https://www2.census.gov/prod2/decennial/documents/1980/1980censusofpopu80150uns_bw.pdf

U.S. Census Bureau. (2020, February 17). *West Virginia Population.* http://worldpopulationreview.com/states/west-virginia/

Wang, S., Rubie-Davies, C. M., & Meissel, K. (2018). A systematic review of the teacher expectation literature over the past 30 years. *Educational Research and Evaluation, 24,* 124–179. doi:10.1080/13803611.2018.1548798

Part II

ASIAN AMERICAN PERSPECTIVES

Beyond Blackness and Whiteness

CHAPTER 6

Like Captured Fireflies

Effective Teaching Pedagogy of a White Elementary School Counselor

Nicholas D. Hartlep

"Like Captured Fireflies" is a poem written by John Steinbeck (1955). In this chapter I draw from the poem when describing the pedagogy of Mr. Smith, a school counselor who helped me as a student. "Deathless power" (line 23) is something Mr. Smith had. He was the 4th-grade counselor at MacArthur Elementary School (Green Bay, Wisconsin), who I saw when my adoptive parents were getting divorced. He was White; he had a full Santa Claus–like beard, and he was patiently gentle when I was experiencing what a 9-year-old adopted Korean boy could not make sense of alone. In this chapter I share how Mr. Smith was a "teacher who wrote on my mind" (line 15, adapted) and how I am his "unsigned manuscript" (line 24). Steinbeck's poem uses the pronoun "she." I know well that elementary teachers are predominantly (75%) women, but male teachers play an important role in elementary schools for students of all genders. Moreover, when the word "teacher" is invoked in the poem, many may think of a general education or a special education teacher. I will argue that in my story, counselors are legitimate teachers. Mythologizing the reality of teaching is something that happens in Steinbeck's poem, but my story attempts to do the opposite. In this autoethnographic chapter I argue that 27 years later, Mr. Smith "left his signature upon me" (line 13, adapted). I am a happily married father of three daughters and am a male teacher educator. I am an endowed professor and department chair at Berea College, a highly progressive liberal arts college in the South that does not charge students tuition. It is my solemn professional duty to prepare teachers to be like Mr. Smith, who "wrote on my mind" (line 15, adapted) and who are tender teachers who listen to the traumas of their students, but who hope for change and transformation.

WHOSE TRAUMA AND WHAT IS TRAUMA?

When teachers and teacher educators hear the word *trauma*, they will most likely think of adverse childhood experiences (ACEs). According to a research brief by Sacks et al. (2014), "Adverse childhood experiences (ACEs) are potentially traumatic events that can have negative, lasting effects on health and well-being. These experiences range from physical, emotional, or sexual abuse to *parental divorce* or the incarceration of a parent or guardian" (p. 1, emphasis added). Highly effective teachers know about ACEs and how to combat them by employing trauma-informed practices (TIPs) (see RB-Banks & Meyer, 2017). Counselors and teachers must be able to deploy TIPs because, as RB-Banks and Meyer (2017) state, "The new face of trauma is often invisible in today's classroom because traditionally childhood trauma is often seen as a domain for social workers or clinical psychologists" (p. 66).

In this chapter, I draw attention to transracial adoptees, an understudied student population when it comes to multicultural education (Pang & Palmer, 2012), and also to a form of ACEs trauma that doesn't receive much attention by practitioners: divorce of adoptive parents. The students in our nation's schools are predominantly poor, and it is a misconception to believe our nation's P–12 students reside in households with two cisgender, heterosexual parents. According to Gretchen Livingston (2014) of the Pew Research Center, "Fewer than half (46%) of U.S. kids younger than 18 years of age are living in a home with two married heterosexual parents in their first marriage." Moreover, the Southern Education Foundation (2013) informs us that the majority of students are poor enough that they qualify for free lunch.

As an adoptee, the divorce of my White, heterosexual, adoptive parents magnified the loss I had already experienced when I was "relinquished" when I was 16 months old on the streets of Seoul, South Korea (Philyaw, 2014). My White, cisgender, heterosexual adoptive parents raised me in the Midwest (Wisconsin). I attended public K–12 schools within the Green Bay Public School District, the first of these being MacArthur Elementary School, which I walked to or biked to every day. The trauma of being a transracially adopted kid in elementary school at MacArthur was difficult to process because most of my classmates and my teachers were White and knew their biological parents. The trauma of experiencing White racism was difficult to bear. Being physically picked on was bad enough, but the emotional wounds of being called a "chink" or a "gook" never seemed to end. Who could I tell these things to, especially when most of the students at the school were White and had racially matching biological parents? Who of my teachers could I confide in?

During my time at MacArthur Elementary School, it was the anti-Asian racism that I experienced during school and the unraveling of my adoptive parents' marriage outside of school that made my life as a 9-year-old human being so difficult. Coming home to an empty house was normal for me—I was a "latchkey" kid. I'd watch episodes of *MacGyver* until my adoptive mother would come home and make dinner. When this routine was interrupted, I knew I needed help, but I didn't know who could help. My adoptive father became more absent. And in his place, a replacement appeared: Jim. Jim was a fireman who also was White, but who liked my adoptive mother (Sue) so much that he would spend a lot of time at my house. During this time, Jim would be at my house, but my adoptive father (Mike) was nowhere to be seen. My adoptive parents were not even officially divorced, yet Jim dared to take me and my mom and soon-to-be stepsister (Kelly) out for ice cream. I had enough of this so that one day I yelled and called Jim a "bastard." My adoptive mother, Sue, reprimanded me when she heard me say this. Her response was a direct message to me that her divorce was something she would not tolerate talking about. My moments of anger were received by her as things I needed to bury and keep hidden from her. In her eyes it was inappropriate for me to express what I was expressing in such a way. And this is how my experiences with racism were. I could not share the racism I experienced because my mother did not want to hear about it. When she did hear me talk about it, she dismissed it as, "They are just being mean." She'd even tell me, "Ignore them."

Research on adoptees confirms that being silenced by adoptive parents is common and routinely experienced (Andriola, 2016). The reason for this finding is that adoptive parents frequently harbor colorblind racial ideologies and communicative tendencies. This was the case with my adoptive mother—who I would label a colorblind racist—evidenced by the fact that she did not consider herself a racist, although she did have a black cat that she named "Sambo." If my adoptive mother wouldn't listen to the trauma I was experiencing, who would and/or could?

Figure 6.1. The Importance of Human Needs in the Learning Process

ELEMENTARY SCHOOL COUNSELOR MR. SMITH

I began seeing Mr. Smith, the school counselor at MacArthur Elementary School, when my parents were separating. I am glad I saw him because Mr. Smith was an effective listener and taught me many things via the counseling sessions he provided me. He helped me learn and process what I was experiencing, but his counseling also helped me when it came to the other subjects I was learning in school. Research by Maslow (1943), Bloom (1956), and others (Dodge et al., 2016), has repeatedly found that students' primary needs (Maslow) must be met before learning objectives can be met (Bloom) (see Figure 6.1). Students will not be able to get to higher levels of thinking if their human needs are not taken care of. The traumatic experiences I was having at home due to the separation of my adoptive parents and not being able to share my experiences with racism was impeding my learning in all of my school subjects (mathematics, science, language arts, and so on), so Mr. Smith's counseling was extremely beneficial to me at the most human level.

Mr. Smith was a powerful male role model for me during a time when my parents were going through a divorce that caused me to not see my adoptive father much (Shears, 2010). While I did see Jim, who would eventually become my stepfather, I could not stand Jim, and Mr. Smith was everything Jim was not. Mr. Smith was nonjudgmental. He was supportive. He was capable of taking perspectives that were not his own. Evidence of Mr. Smith's teaching effectiveness was that his teaching wasn't received as instruction so much as it was always a lesson on life. Although at first I was reluctant to attend counseling with Mr. Smith, in the end, when he told me that I didn't need to see him anymore, I was sad and didn't want to stop seeing him.

After many counseling sessions, when Mr. Smith told me that I was doing well and that I no longer needed to see him, I felt heartache; I had come to look forward to the one-on-one sessions. My sadness abated a little when he told me that he had an open-door policy and that I would always be welcomed in his office. Many times, I would have a case of self-imposed hypochondria—and I would sneak off to the nurse's office only because it offered me a chance to walk past Mr. Smith's office and wave hello. He would always wave hello and that was enough for me.

The major lessons I hope to share in this chapter, based on research as well as on what I learned from Mr. Smith as a teacher, are the following:

- Effective elementary teachers listen and are nonjudgmental.
- Effective elementary teachers don't necessarily solve their students' problems.
- Men make effective elementary teachers.
- Effective elementary teachers are patiently gentle.

EFFECTIVE ELEMENTARY TEACHERS LISTEN AND ARE NONJUDGMENTAL

Scholarly research tells us that effective teachers are nonjudgmental and listen (Haberman, 2004). Research finds that elementary school children are "expected to spend more time . . . listening than any other single activity in the elementary school . . . [yet] teachers are unaware of the amount of time they expect children to listen" (Wilt, 1950, p. 633). These findings illustrate the importance of teachers listening to their students. While it is ideal for elementary school teachers to listen to their students, due to time constraints, curriculum, and other demands, listening can quickly become a luxury in an elementary school classroom. Mr. Smith was one-on-one with me during our counseling sessions, and we frequently had opportunities to go outside, weather permitting, and talk while I swung or played on the jungle gym. The demands and current structure of the school day disallow for a lot of one-on-one time with students, but an implication for preservice and inservice teachers is that this time does exist, if you make it. Preservice teachers, if you are in clinical field experiences, oftentimes you can request tutoring time where you can work in a small group or even one-on-one with a student. This is an opportune time for you to listen to your students. If you are an inservice or practicing teacher, you can "create" time to be one-on-one with a student over your prep period or during your lunch period. You can invite a student to join you for lunch and can listen with fewer interruptions. Supplemental tutoring after school is also a time when you can have one-on-one time with your students.

When it comes to being nonjudgmental, Mr. Smith never judged me for my intense feelings about my stepfather. He also did not judge my adoptive father for divorcing my adoptive mother. Mr. Smith served as a sounding board and "sponge" for me. He listened intently and soaked up all of my processing or venting. By not telling me how to feel, he allowed me to make sense of my trauma and the tension I was experiencing. In our book *What Makes A Star Teacher: 7 Dispositions That Support Student Learning,* my coauthors and I (Hill-Jackson et al., 2019) write that effective teachers seek to understand without judgment. Expressing judgment shuts down communication, trust, and learning. As pointed out earlier, young children are expected to listen so much throughout the day, they yearn to be listened to. As the late Maya Angelou said, "At the end of the day people won't remember what you said or did, they will remember how you made them feel." This is true about Mr. Smith; I don't remember what he said or did, but I remember that he made me feel safe, that I would get through it. And I did!

EFFECTIVE ELEMENTARY TEACHERS DON'T NECESSARILY SOLVE THEIR STUDENTS' PROBLEMS

Myles Horton, the American educator, socialist, and cofounder of the Highlander Folk School, famously said that the poor have the answers. What he meant was that poor people have the solutions to their problems, and that others do not have to "save" the poor. The same logic is true when it comes to teaching. Students do not need their problems solved per se. Effective elementary teachers have no business being "knights" and "solving" their students' life problems. Mr. Smith's pedagogy as a teacher was one of care, compassion, and love, for sure; but when the day was over, he knew I would be going home and re-entering the "dissolving" family structure whether or not he thought it was good for me or not. He had no power over my adoptive parents' marriage, and he didn't want any. Effective teachers understand and take responsibility for the impact that they make during school hours (Haberman, 1995/2004). Mr. Smith helped me by listening to me and engaging in what Paulo Freire (1968/2007) labeled "problem-posing," by which I eventually solved my problems.

One problem I had as an elementary-age student with limited life experience was misunderstanding decisionmaking. When my parents were divorcing one another, I mistakenly thought it was my fault. I mistakenly thought that if I did something better that my adoptive parents would remain in love, and I wouldn't have to have a divorced family. Mr. Smith helped me understand that I was not the reason they were separating. I also learned from Mr. Smith that it was okay for men to cry. As a 9-year-old boy, I was socialized via hegemonic masculinity that crying was socially unacceptable and something to be avoided at all costs.

Mr. Smith encouraged me to cry when I had to and told me it would help me "get it out." Mr. Smith was right—getting my feelings out helped me feel better and heal. Whenever I cried, I felt better after it. Mr. Smith had the wherewithal to know that in sessions where I would cry, that I would need Kleenex; and he would let my tears dry up and my eyes go from red to a more normal color before I returned to the classroom. To me, as a young man, those were thoughtful characteristics that I still hold onto. He knew that if I went back to the class too soon that my red eyes would draw attention to me or embarrass me. This shows Mr. Smith's awareness that he wasn't there to solve my problems so much as to listen to them.

MEN MAKE EFFECTIVE ELEMENTARY TEACHERS

The pedagogy that a teacher has is not necessarily masculine or feminine, although as humans who live in a social world that is gendered and sexed, society may imply that differences do exist. Mr. Smith's pedagogy was one of "presenteeism" and "active listening." He was a gentle giant who encouraged me to cry and get in touch with my intense feelings, without judgment. Men make effective teachers although they are extremely underrepresented. Wong (2019) notes in *The Atlantic* article "The U.S. Teaching Population is Getting Bigger, and More Female" that women now make up a larger share of educators than they have in decades. According to the National Center for Education Statistics (2020), "About 77 percent of public school teachers were female and 23 percent were male in 2015–16, with a lower percentage of male teachers at the elementary school level (11 percent) than at the secondary school level (36 percent)" (para. 2).

Although their study took place in Australia, survey research by McGrath and Sinclair (2013) found that parents considered male elementary school teachers to be important for boy students because they served as role models. Survey research in the United States has returned similar results (see *The Guardian*, 2008). Research by Martino (2008) draws attention to the importance of male teachers yet cautions against over-essentializing teaching as "women's work." Because male elementary teachers, especially male elementary teachers of color, are underrepresented, scholars have begun researching how to best recruit and retain them in the classroom (see Bristol, 2015; Bristol & Mentor, 2018). There are effective male elementary teachers, but one of the challenges that males face as elementary school teachers is societal stereotypes that men are disciplinarians and incapable of working with young children. These gendered challenges seem to reproduce the same shortage the aforementioned scholars are attempting to ameliorate.

EFFECTIVE ELEMENTARY TEACHERS ARE PATIENTLY GENTLE

Martin Haberman (2008) in his famous article "Gentle Teaching in a Violent Society" describes how effective teachers—those he labels as Star Teachers—interact with students gently. The Star Teachers that Haberman (2008) studied practiced "gentle teaching," which included the following:

- Be a source of constant encouragement.
- Demonstrate empathy for students' expressions of feelings.
- Respect students' expressions of ideas.
- Listen, hear, remember, and use students' ideas.

Effective elementary teachers are patiently gentle because, according to Haberman (2008), "a lack of trust in adults naturally makes young children suspicious of adults' motives and actions" (p. 239). Building relationships with students takes time on the part of the teacher and requires patience. Mr. Smith was always positive when he spoke with me. He demonstrated empathy, by sharing that he did not know how parents who divorced would feel because his parents were still married, yet he told me that he most likely would feel sad. He listened. And he waited for me to process and respond to his empathy. Mr. Smith showed me respect as a 9-year-old and actively listened to me.

Research conducted by Thompson et al. (2008) found that patience was a quality associated with outstanding teaching. The researchers surveyed 101 K–12 public school teachers and 271 African American high school seniors regarding the characteristics of outstanding teachers. Their results revealed six qualities that both teachers and students agree are characteristics of outstanding teachers; patience was the second most agreed-upon characteristic by students and teachers.

Being gentle as a teacher is an equally important disposition for elementary teachers to have because of the ages of their students. Because elementary school students are forming their self-development and self-esteem, teachers must be mindful and aware that what they say and how they say it can have consequences on this development. This is why these dispositions are valued, encouraged, and developed when preservice teachers participate in teacher preparation education (see Sherman, 2006). Mr. Smith was quick to listen and slow to speak with me, which epitomizes gentle teaching pedagogy.

COMING FULL CIRCLE

My circle must return to where it began. John Steinbeck's poem "Like Captured Fireflies" has a verse that reads, "She left her signature upon us" (line 13), which resonates with me now as a 37-year-old transracial (Asian American) adoptee teacher educator. Although I was with Mr. Smith for a mere year, Mr. Smith has been with me for 28 years. Mr. Smith "created in me a new thing"(line 19), and that thing is an inner peace. As a married adult and father of three daughters, I now know that my adoptive parents' divorce had nothing to do with me, and everything to do with them. I would not be who I am personally or professionally without the cumulative experiences I have had, and as a teacher educator, I have learned a lot about myself and others from Mr. Smith, an elementary school counselor. I do believe that the experiences of adopted children have been woefully absent in all forms of literature, including scholarly, and I am blessed to be able to add mine to the silence. And whatever happened to Mr. Smith? I can only believe that he is now retired, since if my math is correct, he would be around 67 years old at the time of this writing. If Mr. Smith only knew the "deathless power" (line 23) that he helped fortify in me.

Sincerely,
Unsigned manuscript (line 24)

REFERENCES

Andriola, T. (2016, July 20). *5 times I have felt silenced in adoption.* https://adoption.com/5-times-felt-silenced-adoption-adoptee-perspective/

Bloom, B. S. (1956). *Taxonomy of educational objectives.* Allyn and Bacon.

Bristol, T. J. (2015). Male teachers of color take a lesson from each other. *Phi Delta Kappan, 97*(2), 36–41.

Bristol, T. J., & Mentor, M. (2018). Policing and teaching: The positioning of Black male teachers as agents in the universal carceral apparatus. *The Urban Review, 50,* 218–234.

Dodge, D. T., Berke, K., Baker, H., & Bickart, T. S. (2016). *The creative curriculum for preschool.* Teaching Strategies.

Freire, P. (2007). *Pedagogy of the Oppressed.* Continuum. (Original work published 1968)

Haberman, M. (2004). *Star teachers of children in poverty.* Haberman Educational Foundation. (Original work published 1995)

Haberman, M. (2004). *Teacher talk.* Haberman Educational Foundation.

Haberman, M. (2008). Gentle teaching in a violent society. *Educational Horizons, 86,* 238–248. (Original work published 1994) https://files.eric.ed.gov/fulltext/EJ798524.pdf

Hill-Jackson, V., Hartlep, N. D., & Stafford, D. (2019). *What makes a Star Teacher: 7 dispositions that support student learning.* Association for the Supervision of Curriculum and Development.

Livingston, G. (2014, December 22). Fewer than half of U.S. kids today live in a "traditional" family. *Pew Research Center.* http://www.pewresearch.org/fact-tank/2014/12/22/less-than-half-of-u-s-kids-today-live-in-a-traditional-family/

Martino, W. J. (2008). Male teachers as role models: Addressing issues of masculinity, pedagogy, and the re-masculinization of schooling. *Curriculum Inquiry, 38*(2), 189–223.

Maslow, A. (1943). A theory of human motivation. *Psychological Review, 50*(4), 370–396.

McGrath, K., & Sinclair, M. (2013). More male primary-school teachers? Social benefits for boys and girls. *Gender and Education, 25*(5), 531–547.

National Center for Education Statistics. (2020). Characteristics of public school teachers. In *The condition of education.* https://nces.ed.gov/programs/coe/indicator_clr.asp

Pang, V. O., & Palmer, J. D. (2012). Model minorities and the model minority myth. In J. A. Banks (Ed.), *Encyclopedia of Diversity in Education* (Vol. 3, p. 1518). Sage Publications.

Philyaw, D. (2014, January 12). When divorce magnifies adoption's losses. *Motherlode* (Blog). *The New York Times.* https://parenting.blogs.nytimes.com/2014/01/12/when-divorce-magnifies-adoptions-losses/

RB-Banks, Y., & Meyer, J. (2017). Childhood trauma in today's classroom: Moving beyond the therapist's office. *The Journal of Educational Foundations, 30*(1–4), 63–75.

Sacks, V., Murphey, D., & Moore, K. (2014, July). *Adverse childhood experiences: National and state-level prevalence* [Research brief]. Child Trends. https://www.childtrends.org/wp-content/uploads/2014/07/Brief-adverse-childhood-experiences_FINAL.pdf

Shears, J. (2010). Benefits of a male's presence in the classroom. *NHSA Dialog, 13*(1), 66–70.

Sherman, S. (2006). Moral dispositions in teacher education: Making them matter. *Teacher Education Quarterly, 33*(4), 41–57. https://files.eric.ed.gov/fulltext/EJ795225.pdf

Southern Education Foundation. (2013, October). *A new majority: Low income students in the South and nation.* https://www.southerneducation.org/wp-content/uploads/2019/02/New-Majority-2013.pdf

Steinbeck, J. (1955). Like captured fireflies. http://www.alisonpask.de/wp-content/uploads/2012/08/john-steinbeck-like-catpured-fireflies.pdf

The Guardian. (2008, September 29). Male teachers are crucial role models for boys, suggests research. https://www.theguardian.com/education/2008/sep/30/primaryschools.malerolemodels

Thompson, G. L., Warren, S. R., Foy, T., & Dickerson, C. (2008). What makes a teacher outstanding? A contrast of teachers' and African American high school students' perspectives. *Journal of Urban Learning, Teaching, and Research, 4,* 122–134. http://citeseerx.ist.psu.edu/viewdoc/download?doi=10.1.1.1024.5745&rep=rep1&type=pdf

Wilt, M. E. (1950). A study of teacher awareness of listening as a factor in elementary education. *The Journal of Educational Research, 43*(8), 626–636.

Wong, A. (2019, February 20). The U.S. teaching population is getting bigger, and more female. *The Atlantic.* https://www.theatlantic.com/education/archive/2019/02/the-explosion-of-women-teachers/582622/

CHAPTER 7

Finding My Voice

Developing a Critical Writing and APIDA Identity in a Newspaper Course

Theodore Chao

I identify as a Chinese American mathematics teacher educator, in solidarity with the larger social identity of Asian Pacific Islander Desi American (APIDA) teacher educators. My teacher education scholarship revolves around issues of power and privilege. I engage teachers in paying attention to the way race, gender, socioeconomic status, and other social constructs affect their relationships with students. My passion for engaging teachers in these critical conversations comes from personal experiences in which I recall very few teachers engaged in honest conversations about race and power with me. This chapter describes one teacher, Ms. Janice Cummons, who explicitly spoke about issues of power as related to race. Ms. Cummons's pedagogy significantly impacted my academic journey, leading me to recognize how Whiteness was centered in my own mathematics teaching and then how to critique this racism and privilege.

In high school I was sheltered from conversations about race or culture. I was a 2nd-generation Chinese American growing up within a bubble of privilege. Almost all my teachers were White. Almost all my peer interactions were with White or 2nd-generation Chinese American and Taiwanese American peers from families who held substantial socioeconomic privilege. I enjoyed playing basketball, football, and tennis. I was active in a student group named Republican Youth. And I tried so hard to distance myself from stereotypes connected to the model minority myth that I did not participate in extracurricular mathematics even though I loved mathematics. This is who I was when I met Ms. Cummons in 1993, the spring of my 10th-grade year.

At the time, Ms. Cummons was in her 15th year as a high school teacher. Ms. Cummons, who identifies as White, had grown up in a working-class family in a largely White community outside of Detroit. Because of the lack of diversity in her childhood community and in the school she would work in, she admits that she initially took a standard colorblind approach to teaching by trying not to see anyone's race and treating all students as equal (Banks, 1989; Matias & Zembylas, 2014).

When I was in high school, our school newspaper was a monthly, tabloid-sized newsprint, written and edited completely by students. Ms. Cummons served as the faculty advisor, but rarely interjected into the newspaper's editorial decisions. Ms. Cummons's pedagogical philosophy involved giving students considerable freedom to run the newspaper autonomously, to write articles meaningful to their own school and community, and to connect with their local community. As a journalism teacher, she wanted to help students find their writing voice and build off the confidence that comes from seeing your name in print. She allowed students the power to write about what was important to them with only one warning: Do not get her sued or fired. I took ownership of my role on the newspaper staff, using it to learn how to serve my school and local community and to hone my writing voice.

THEORETICAL FRAMEWORK

AsianCrit

AsianCrit, a subset of Critical Race Theory (Delgado & Stefancic, 2012; Ladson-Billings & Tate, 2006), delves into the ways that race and racism affect APIDAs, particularly in light of the ways White supremacy is normalized within the United States (Museus & Iftikar, 2013). In this chapter, I focus on three tenets of AsianCrit: (1) Asianization; (2) Story, Theory, and Praxis; and (3) Commitment to Social Justice (Museus & Iftikar, 2013).

First, *Asianization* describes the ways that APIDAs are often lumped together as a monolithic entity in order to perpetuate racist stereotypes. For instance, the model minority myth stereotype positions APIDAs as obedient, hardworking, and particularly adept at mathematics and science in order to discredit other communities of color (Chen & Buell, 2017/2018; Hartlep, 2013). Asianization also emasculates APIDA men, positioning them as generally stoic, nonsexual, and uncreative (Eng, 2001). Second, *Story, Theory, and Praxis* acknowledges the ways counterstories, theoretical work, and practice connect to analyze and advocate for the APIDA experience (Museus & Iftikar, 2013). Counterstories and counternarratives amplify the voices of APIDAs that speak out against colonization and its effects on the APIDA community (Solorzano & Yosso, 2002; Yeh et al., 2019). Third, a *Commitment to Social Justice* advocates for an end to all forms of oppression, particularly along intersecting systems of subordination such as racism, sexism, hetorosexism, and capitalism (Museus & Iftikar, 2013). In conjunction with the other tenets of AsianCrit, a commitment to social justice means that APIDA stories have the power to recognize and advocate against oppressive systems, bringing to light systems of power that invisibly oppress APIDAs (Chen & Buell, 2017/2018; Coloma, 2006; Poon, 2014; Teranishi et al., 2009).

Mathematics Teacher Identity and Voice

My work as a mathematics teacher educator involves engaging mathematics teachers to develop positive mathematics identities that intersect with their teacher identities (Kalinec-Craig et al., 2019; Marshall & Chao, 2017; McCloskey et al., 2017). I recognize mathematics teachers as identity workers, an identity in which they help students see themselves as mathematical beings (Gutiérrez, 2013).

Exploring one's own mathematics teacher identity involves negotiating personal, cultural, and community stories with professional responsibilities and narratives (Chao, 2014; de Freitas, 2008). This builds on the AsianCrit tenet of Story, Theory, and Praxis, in which mathematics teacher identity involves the telling and retelling of counterstories (Museus & Iftikar, 2013; Solorzano & Yosso, 2002). These counterstories help teachers reflect on how they either confront or reify oppressive practices that exist within traditional mathematics teaching, such as ability grouping or Eurocentric curricula (Gutiérrez, 2013; Herbel-Eisenmann et al., 2013). When mathematics teachers tell and retell their stories, they hone their voice to call out injustice in mathematics education.

Teacher Effectiveness

Within mathematics teacher education, *teacher effectiveness* encompasses the ways a teacher actively helps students not only develop effective mathematical practices (National Governors Association Center for

Best Practices & Council of Chief State School Officers, 2010), but also how teachers help students develop positive mathematics identities (Kalinec-Craig et al., 2019). Teacher effectiveness, therefore, involves teachers developing authentic relationships with students through praxis, engaging students to connect their mathematical critique with justification and action (Gutstein, 2006). In this way, teacher effectiveness can be thought of as not just helping students find their mathematical voice, but also in helping them learn to recognize and take action against injustice (Chao et al., 2014).

MS. CUMMONS'S TEACHER EFFECTIVENESS

I first met Ms. Janice Cummons when she met with me to read some of my writing to determine whether I could skip her Introduction to Journalism class and move directly into Newspaper, a separate course reserved for the newspaper staff. Ms. Cummons looked through my writing samples and talked with several of my peers and teachers before allowing me to join the newspaper staff during my 11th-grade year. I was thrilled to directly join the newspaper staff and enroll in a daily 47-minute course that revolved around putting out a new issue of the newspaper every month.

First, this early recognition of my writing ability had a large impact on my emerging voice. At the time, I felt that most of my teachers positioned me within the fictive dichotomy of logical left-brain versus creative right-brain. This categorization was probably based on my high grades in mathematics and my teachers' belief in the model minority myth, which positions APIDA students as having an innate mathematics ability (Hartlep, 2013; Lee, 1996). Ms. Cummons was the first teacher to ignore this positioning and see my emerging writing ability.

Second, Ms. Cummons encouraged writing stories that mattered to us, allowing us to take ownership of our narratives. I remember the nervousness of cold calling a story source and leaving a detailed voice message about calling back during the small time window I would be next to the newspaper phone. (This was 1994, a time before email and mobile phones.) Within a school setting filled with bell schedules, busywork, and an overemphasis on obedience, the freedom that Ms. Cummons's Newspaper course allowed me to experience what Freire (1968/1970) referred to a "problem-posing education" for the first time. I got to write stories through listening to the voices of everyone involved.

Third, Ms. Cummons encouraged me to write. Before Newspaper, I had never positioned myself as a writer. I loved sports, video games, math, and science, in that order. And while I was always reading a book and was active in my school's extemporaneous speaking team, I never felt that I was a "writer." Much of this was racialized. I was Chinese American. I felt social pressures to excel in the fields I was "supposed to," like mathematics, science, and engineering. I saw few APIDA role models who were writers or made a living in creative enterprise. So, it never occurred to me that *I* could be a writer too.

But in Newspaper, I was a journalist. I wrote stories. I voiced community concerns. I spoke my truth. I no longer felt like a tolerated visitor to my own community, positioned as a forever foreigner (Tuan, 1998). Now, through my writing, I was speaking *for* my community. Ms. Cummons's philosophy that the newspaper should be something we, as the newspaper staff, were proud of because we created it ourselves resonated with me. These were *my* stories about *my* world.

When our monthly newspaper came out, teachers and students would compliment my writing, which made me realize how much I enjoyed getting published. My early stories recapped the tennis team's season, highlighted resources available in the library, and the school's production of *The Music Man*. Quickly, my writing grew to cover things that mattered to me: Björk's solo debut, the state of the NBA after Michael Jordan's retirement, and my critique of the public ranking of student grade point averages, particularly because of the imperfect mathematics behind these calculations. Through my 11th- and 12th-grade years, I learned how to use the newspaper to engage in public discourse around issues in my world. I also started writing satirical pieces. I wrote a fake advice column giving nonsensical advice to high schoolers from the conservative, southern, Christian point of view that dominated our school's culture. I crafted fake advertisements for albums and products that did not exist to mock a retail industry trying to sell "alternative" as a commercial lifestyle. I made a fake children's menu pull-out filled with subtle, racial aggressions to mock the White supremacist messages aimed toward children that my childhood was filled with. I wrote serious pieces too. I remember winning a student journalism award for a stream-of-consciousness reflection describing my shock and hurt feelings surrounding a classmate's suicide. I learned to see the power of writing and how to use multiple voices to draw attention to things that did not feel right.

REVIEWING THE JOY LUCK CLUB

Amy Tan's book, *The Joy Luck Club*, was a powerful experience for me when I read it in high school. I remember the dizzying emotions it evoked with real, multidimensional APIDA characters who, like me, struggled to navigate the space between two cultures. So much from my own life was in this book: the Chinese Baptist Church, the melodic tones of Cantonese permeating every meal, the judgmental stereotypes perpetuated onto the White men who married into our family, and the mother–daughter relationships that had to navigate both sexism and racism. These stories mirrored my own stories.

But I did not have anyone around me to talk about *The Joy Luck Club* with. None of my school peers read the book like I did; they only wanted to talk about the "exotic" Chinese American culture revealed in the book through "tourist" eyes (Tuan, 1998). And none of my male APIDA friends admitted to reading *The Joy Luck Club*. We had already learned how to put on the mask of toxic masculinity to combat the emasculation we felt (Eng, 2001). We did not want to admit reading a "chick lit" book. So, filled with this tension of loving *The Joy Luck Club* book, but not having space to discuss my feelings, I attended a press screening of *The Joy Luck Club* film. I was going to review *The Joy Luck Club* film for the school newspaper.

I loved the film. I cried. I pretended I wasn't crying. I cried again. The movie took me to a magical place where the stories about my family, my cousins, my uncles, my aunts, and the intricate Chinese and American traditions we held around food, money, school, and each other were finally told. For the first time, everyone had a window into my world. And I had the privilege to write about it for my high school community. I wanted to write something as beautiful as this film made me feel.

But I made the mistake of letting other voices into my head. I started reading outside reviews of *The Joy Luck Club*. I grew angry reading these glowing reviews and how it seemed everyone suddenly had appreciation of Chinese American culture. Really? Where was this appreciation during my lunchbox moments in which I was chided for bringing braised tofu to school? Where was this appreciation every single time I was picked last in pick-up basketball because of stereotypes about my athleticism? The glowing reviews made me angry; they seemed to dismiss the deep history of anti-APIDA sentiment in our country (Takaki, 1998).

In my heart, I wrote a review in which I bared my soul on paper with a thoughtful love letter to Amy Tan and Wayne Wang. But I was in high school. I was still dealing with the identity politics of assimilating into a predominantly White space, trying to position myself to my teachers in ways they could understand and not stereotype, and not ready to engage in speaking my whole truth. I did not have many teachers who saw me for me and not my ethnicity.

I ended up writing a rushed review that largely tried to shock, to belittle the work done for this film, to focus on what it was not, and to express anger at the emotional heartstrings it pulled on me. I wrote my review aimed at the White people who used *The Joy Luck Club* as a shallow tool for diversity, yet remain ignorant of how they continued to enact violence through *Asianization* and reifying the model minority myth (Hartlep, 2013; Museus & Iftikar, 2013). I wrote my review to attack the White audiences who loved *The Joy Luck Club*, yet still viewed Chinese and Chinese American as the same. I wrote my review to lash out at the media espousing a narrative that this film would open doors for APIDA actors and filmmakers, knowing that the actors would still have to spend their careers speaking with demeaning accents, playing sex workers, geishas, or emasculated nerds. I used my review to express my anger, frustration, and confusion as an APIDA man.

Ms. Cummons encouraged me to publish this review as I wrote it. She did not ask me to soften the angry tone. She let me explore this anger in confronting the racism I felt all around me. I was not angry at *The Joy Luck Club*. But I was angry at the lack of real conversation about it. I was angry that my own identity as APIDA and the racial politics I saw so clearly in our school and community were not recognized. And I was glad to have this space to vent, to find my voice that could talk about racism and power.

Having a space to write this angry review of *The Joy Luck Club* allowed me to express my raw emotions about my APIDA identity and explore the cathartic action of putting my frustration into public words. From then on, Ms. Cummons helped me learn how to engage in critical conversations and explicitly recognize and confront abuses of power where I saw them. Ms. Cummons's effectiveness as a teacher was creating a system in which I was allowed to write about what I felt, to share my anger and emotions through print, and to use these tools to find my voice.

A TEACHER ACTUALLY TALKING ABOUT RACE

One particular memory I have of Ms. Cummons was on the day she returned to school after taking parental leave to adopt a newborn. I remember we passed a photograph of her growing family around the room. Her baby girl's brown skin and black hair stood out compared to the pale skin of the rest of her family. I had little experience with adoption, let alone transracial adoption. From my other classes, I learned you were not supposed to talk about or acknowledge race. I passed the photo to Paul, a White student, who made an under-the-breath comment, "Hey, your baby's Black. Better make sure you teach her how to apply for food stamps."

A sleep-deprived Ms. Cummons heard the comment. Her face flushed red and her smile disappeared. "What did you say, Paul? Are you making racist comments about my daughter? Do you think it's okay to say that sort of thing because I'm White?"

Paul bowed his head and looked like he wanted to be anywhere else than there. We all sat there shocked. We had not seen Ms. Cummons for a few weeks and were immediately thrust into an intense discussion about race, racism, and why casual racism is still racism. This talk lasted less than 10 minutes, but I'll remember it forever. Paul sat there, avoiding eye-contact. As it happened, I realized that, for the first time in my education, a teacher was actually talking about racism, calling out a racist comment with anger, and honestly showing us how much it hurt her. She did not tell us not to be racist. She did not engage us in a fluff talk about being colorblind. Instead, she asked us to think about the world her child would grow up in, to comprehend how hurtful these "normalized" racist comments were. The part that struck me the hardest was that, while Paul's comment was mean-spirited, his thoughts were not that different from the ways many of us had been taught to think about race—myself included. I realized I too had a lot of growing to do because of this talk we had.

Over the next 2 years, Ms. Cummons would make comments about her struggles in mothering a Black daughter: the stares she got in public, the helplessness she felt in working with her daughter's hair, and her frustration in finding cartoon characters and dolls that looked like her daughter. I got to see, up close, how a White adult was learning about and processing the insidiousness of White supremacy in our society (Delgado & Stefancic, 2012; Ladson-Billings & Tate, 2006). And I appreciated her honest talk with us about her growing frustration.

Ms. Cummons was the first adult I ever met who was so public about her adoption story, particularly in the way she spoke about the racial difference between her and her daughter. Ms. Cummons did not feel the need to explain anything to anyone, particularly if it came from a tone of judgmental White supremacy. I learned a lot from watching Ms. Cummons's evolution. First, I learned that our voices and worldviews can always grow. Second, I learned how to call out racism when I saw it. Third, I learned that the only way to confront racism was not to take a colorblind approach, which every other teacher seemed to do, but to talk about it directly and acknowledge how it made you feel.

MY TEACHER EDUCATION PHILOSOPHY

Today, as a mathematics teacher educator, I center my pedagogy on rehumanizing the craft of mathematics teaching in order to help teachers develop critical lenses and find their voice as mathematics teachers. These are values I trace back to Ms. Cummons.

First, Ms. Cummons's pedagogy showed me that developing your voice takes time. She allowed me space to work through my identity struggles through my writing, to find my voice, even if it meant a nonsensical, angry critique of *The Joy Luck Club* in order to get to a deeper counternarrative about anti-APIDA racism. Second, Ms. Cummons showed me how to call out injustice where I saw it. As a teacher educator, I want my teachers to recognize the many ways mathematics has been and continues to be used to exploit and oppress certain peoples, such as creating economically justified arguments for colonization. Every time I engage in critical conversations in my teaching, I think of Ms. Cummons's honest outburst in which she invited us to try to understand the racial tension she felt raising her daughter. Finally, in today's digital age, I encourage my teachers to continually build, cultivate, and revise their online identities through crafting their online stories (Chao, 2014). My teachers' emerging confidence, which arises from putting their pedagogical ideas in public forums such as Twitter, is exactly what I learned to do in Ms. Cummons's course, through writing imperfect articles that quickly got published. Overall, Ms. Cummons's effectiveness on me as a student, helping me learn how to explore my voice, call out racial injustice, and gain confidence in publishing my work, is the reason I am the critical teacher educator I am today.

CONCLUSION

Ms. Cummons's teaching helped me develop my identity as a critical teacher educator, which I outline through the AsianCrit tenets of (1) Asianization, (2) Story, Theory, and Praxis, and (3) Commitment to Social Justice (Museus & Iftikar, 2013). In high school, I felt bombarded by the many negative stereotypes about Asian Americans. But through Ms. Cummons's willingness to engage in talk about race, I started on a pathway that realized racial stereotypes do not have to define me. This was a critical way for me to recognize the destructive power of Asianization in my life. And, through Ms. Cummons's philosophy of allowing students' to use the school newspaper to find their voice, I was able to craft stories and counterstories about my experiences and create my own critical theory and praxis. And it was through her example as a White adoptive mother who spoke openly about learning to recognize her own privilege that I was able to develop my own teaching to revolve around a commitment to social justice.

Through reflecting on Ms. Cummons's impact on my own pedagogy, I suggest a few recommendations for teachers, both preservice and inservice, to develop their own critical pedagogy. First, teachers need spaces to think through the many stereotypes they have encountered, not only about the children they serve, but also about themselves. This can be done through role playing confrontational scenarios, such as when a colleague expresses doubt as to the racist nature of traditional mathematics teaching practices (Marshall et al., 2019). Second, teachers need to have a space to create their own stories and counterstories in order to cultivate identities as teachers that connect with their many other social identities. This can be done through photovoice narratives in which teachers share and narrate personal photographs (Chao, 2014) and the gradual cultivation of online teacher identities (Vakil & Chao, 2019). Finally, mathematics teachers need opportunities to define teacher effectiveness as developing authentic relationships with students in order to frame their practice around recognizing and taking action against injustice. This can be done through framing mathematics tasks around the situations that come directly from childrens' community funds of knowledge (Aguirre et al., 2013; Chao & Jones, 2016). These recommendations are just some of the many ways Ms. Cummons's teaching impacted me as a critical mathematics teacher educator.

REFERENCES

Aguirre, J. M., Turner, E. E., Bartell, T. G., Kalinec-Craig, C., Foote, M. Q., McDuffie, A. R., & Drake, C. (2013). Making connections in practice: How prospective elementary teachers connect to children's mathematical thinking and community funds of knowledge in mathematics instruction. *Journal of Teacher Education, 64*(2), 178–192. (Published online December 5, 2012) https://doi.org/10.1177%2F0022487112466900

Banks, J. A. (1989). Approaches to multicultural curriculum reform. In J. A. Banks & C. A. Mcgee Banks (Eds.), *Multicultural Education: Issues and Perspectives* (3rd ed., pp. 229–250). John Wiley & Sons.

Chao, T. (2014). Photo-Elicitation/Photovoice interviews to study mathematics teacher identity. In J. Cai, J. Middleton, & L. Van Zoest (Eds.), *Current research in mathematics teacher education: Contributions by PME-NA researchers* (pp. 93–113). Springer.

Chao, T., & Jones, D. (2016). That's not fair and why: Developing social justice mathematics activists in pre–K. *Teaching for Excellence and Equity in Mathematics, 7*(1), 15–21.

Chao, T., Murray, E. C., & Gutiérrez, R. (2014). What are classroom practices that support equity-based mathematics teaching? [NCTM Equity Pedagogy Research Brief]. *National Council of Teachers of Mathematics.* https://www.nctm.org/Research-and-Advocacy/Research-Brief-and-Clips/Classroom-Practices-That-Support-Equity-Based-Mathematics-Teaching/

Chen, G. A., & Buell, J. Y. (2018). Of models and myths: Asian(Americans) in STEM and the neoliberal racial project. *Race Ethnicity and Education, 21*(5), 607–625. (Published online September 20, 2017) https://doi.org/10.1080/13613324.2017.1377170

Coloma, R. S. (2006). Disorienting race and education: Changing paradigms on the schooling of Asian Americans and Pacific Islanders. *Race Ethnicity and Education, 9*(1), 1–15. https://doi.org/10.1080/13613320500490606

de Freitas, E. (2008). Enacting identity through narrative: Interrupting the procedural discourse in mathematics classrooms. In T. Brown (Ed.), *The psychology of mathematics education: A psychoanalytic displacement* (pp. 139–158). SensePublishers–Rotterdam.

Delgado, R., & Stefancic, J. (2012). *Critical race theory: An introduction.* NYU Press.

Eng, D. L. (2001). *Racial castration: Managing masculinity in Asian America.* Duke University Press.

Freire, P. (1970). *Pedagogy of the oppressed* (30th anniversary ed). Continuum. (Original work published 1968)

Gutiérrez, R. (2013). The sociopolitical turn in mathematics education. *Journal for Research in Mathematics Education, 44,* 37–68.

Gutstein, E. (2006). *Reading and writing the world with mathematics: Toward a pedagogy for social justice.* Routledge.

Hartlep, N. D. (2013). *The model minority stereotype: Demystifying Asian American success.* IAP.

Herbel-Eisenmann, B., Bartell, T. G., Breyfogle, M. L., Bieda, K., Crespo, S., Dominguez, H., & Drake, C. (2013). Strong is the silence: Challenging interlocking systems of privilege and oppression in mathematics teacher education. *Journal of Urban Mathematics Education, 6*(1), 6–18. https://doi.org/10.21423/jume-v6i1a212

Kalinec-Craig, C., Chao, T., Maldonado, L. A., & Celedón-Pattichis, S. (2019). Reflecting back to move forward: Using the mathematics autobiography to open humanizing learning spaces for pre-service mathematics teachers. In T. G. Bartell, C. Drake, A. R. McDuffie, J. M. Aguirre, E. E. Turner, & M. Q. Foote (Eds.), *Transforming Mathematics Teacher Education* (pp. 135–146). Springer. https://link.springer.com/chapter/10.1007/978-3-030-21017-5_10

Ladson-Billings, G., & Tate, W. F. (2006). Toward a critical race theory of education. In A. D. Dixson & C. K. Rousseau (Eds.), *Critical race theory in education: All God's children got a song* (pp. 11–30). Routledge.

Lee, S. J. (1996). *Unraveling the "model minority" stereotype: Listening to Asian American youth.* Teachers College Press.

Marshall, A. M., & Chao, T. (2017). Using mathematics autobiography stories to support emerging elementary mathematics teachers' sociopolitical consciousness and identity. In S. E. Kastberg, A. M. Tyminski, A. E. Lischka, & W. B. Sanchez (Eds.), *Building support for scholarly practices in mathematics methods* (pp. 279–293). Information Age.

Marshall, A. M., McCloskey, A., Lawler, B., & Chao, T. (2019). *"Math is racist now? You don't believe that, do you?" Supporting courageous conversations* [Paper presentation]. Association of Mathematics Teacher Educators Annual Meeting, Orlando, Florida.

Matias, C. E., & Zembylas, M. (2014). "When saying you care is not really caring": Emotions of disgust, whiteness ideology, and teacher education. *Critical Studies in Education, 55*(3), 319–337. https://doi.org/10.1080/17508487.2014.922489

McCloskey, A., Lawler, B. R., & Chao, T. (2017). The "mirror test:" A tool for reflection on our sociopolitical identities as mathematics teacher educators. In S. E. Kastberg, A. M. Tyminski, A. E. Lischka, & W. B. Sanchez (Eds.), *Building support for scholarly practices in mathematics methods* (pp. 325–339). Information Age.

Museus, S. D., & Iftikar, J. (2013). An Asian critical theory (AsianCrit) framework. In M. Y. Danico & J. G. Golson (Eds.), *Asian American students in higher education* (pp. 18–29). Routledge.

National Governors Association Center for Best Practices & Council of Chief State School Officers. (2010). *Standards for mathematical practice.* Common Core State Standards Initiative. http://www.corestandards.org/Math/Practice/

Poon, O. (2014). "The land of opportunity doesn't apply to everyone": The immigrant experience, race, and Asian American career choices. *Journal of College Student Development, 55*(6), 499–514. https://doi.org/10.1353/csd.2014.0056

Solorzano, D. G., & Yosso, T. J. (2002). A critical race counterstory of race, racism, and affirmative action. *Equity & Excellence in Education, 35*(2), 155–168.

Takaki, R. (1998). *Strangers from a different shore: A history of Asian Americans* (Updated and revised). Little, Brown and Company.

Teranishi, R. T., Behringer, L. B., Grey, E. A., & Parker, T. L. (2009). Critical race theory and research on Asian Americans and Pacific Islanders
in higher education. *New Directions for Institutional Research* (142), 57–68.
https://doi.org/10.1002/ir.296

Tuan, M. (1998). *Forever foreigners or honorary whites? The Asian ethnic experience
today*. Rutgers University Press.

Vakil, J., & Chao, T. (2019). Mathematics teacher education in the age of
Twitter: A critical tool in elementary math methods. In S. Otten, A. G.
Candela, Z. de Araujo, C. Haines, & C. Munter (Eds.), *Proceedings of the
forty-first annual meeting of the North American Chapter of the International
Group for the Psychology of Mathematics Education* (pp. 1289–1294). Univer-
sity of Missouri.

Yeh, C., Louie, N. L., Kokka, K., Jong, C., Eli, J. A., Chao, T., & Adiredja,
A. P. (2019). *Growing against the grain: Counterstories of Asian American
mathematics education scholars* [Roundtable session]. American Educational Research Association Annual Meeting, Toronto, ON, Canada.

Part III

NATIVE AMERICAN PERSPECTIVES

Indigeneity Is Not Race

CHAPTER 8

"The Moon Will Tell Us When It Will Rain"

Aesthetics of Grandmothers' Pedagogies

Amanda R. Tachine

I am a Navajo woman raised in the beauty of *Lo'kaah ni teel* (patch of wide reeds), also referred to as Ganado, Arizona. During the summer months and on Sundays, as a child and into a teenager, you often found me with my grandmothers at church gatherings. They were viewed as being in charge of preparing the food, but they did more than that. They were the behind-the-scenes women organizing for the community. Corn stew, frybread, grilled mutton, tortillas, and so many more dishes were created in their homes, the tiny kitchen at the church, or the fired grill on top of the mountain at Fluted Rock. While food was cooking, conversations were happening on who will be speaking that night, which families were going through tough times and ways to support them, and also plans for the next and the next and the next community gatherings. They were showing me a matrilineal way of life, in a world that prides itself on patriarchy. There was Grandma Carole (my mother's aunt), a strong stubborn matriarch. She was a natural leader who knew how to organize and get things done. I admired those qualities in her, and so I did everything she asked me to do. I washed the dishes, helped make bread, served coffee, and picked up the trash outside. And I felt a sense of pride when she acknowledged my work with a cold soda. There was her younger sister Grandma Caroline, a silly and kind matriarch who to this day makes me laugh. She was in the kitchen with us too, often taking orders from Carole and making quiet jokes as she walked by me. Her sense of humor is contagious, and, as I learned Native humor from her, I would be ready to respond back to her with a clever comment. We went back and forth, back and forth, until we were both wiping

91

our eyes with tears because we were laughing so hard. I called her recently, and we started talking about having a party in the hospital. She was battling a sickness and missing home while being in the hospital for days too long. When I learned that she was there amidst the chlorine stench and too bright fluorescent lights of the hospital, I called her. I wanted to make her laugh, make her feel a little better. We bantered, teased, and giggled through the phone, and then she told me, "Mandy, I know God has everything under control. I am okay. I am not afraid." Those words rang true as Grandma Caroline has an unshakable amount of faith, a quality that I admire.

Then there was my *"shimasani,"* my mother's mother, Dorothy. Typing her name now makes me quiver as warm tears move down my face. Shimasani was the oldest sister and the unspoken leader of the family. A naturally loving matriarch, Shimasani was often quiet, calm, and relentlessly devoted. I rarely heard her speak negatively of people. The only time I remember her being upset was when my cousin started stealing and lying to her. Shimasani was frustrated for sure about her missing items, but I think she was more concerned about my cousin and the choices she was making at such an early age. Shimasani loved my cousin, loved us, loved everyone, and that love was felt. I can still feel that love even after she crossed over nearly 17 years ago. In thinking about a teacher who influenced me, I thought of all my grandmothers, but for today I will share most of her, Shimasani. I return to her ways in so many facets of my life, as a mother of three, as a teacher to countless students, as a writer and scholar, and as a relative and stranger to many. She helped me to develop grandmothers' pedagogies (Tachine, 2017) that personify aesthetic indigeneity and are rooted in Indigenous knowledge systems of love, spirituality, sustenance, and kinship. Grandmothers' pedagogies are lessons learned from Grandma Carole, Grandma Caroline, and Shimasani, teachings that are in the margins of most conversations about schooling and education. These are teachings that have sustained us as *Diné* (Navajo) people for generations; such culturally sustaining pedagogies are about "sustaining cultures as connected to sustaining the bodies—the lives—of the people who cherish and practice them" (Paris & Alim, 2017).

LEARNING THE NAVAJO WAYS FROM SHIMASANI

Before kindergarten and formal schooling, each morning my mom woke my siblings and me up early, rushed us out the door, and drove us on the dirt road to our grandpa and grandma's house. We were on our way to schooling by grandparents. They lived on top of a hill where the soil had deep shades of purple, gray, maroon, and brown, where the juniper trees stood with power and released sweet fragrance especially after the rain blessed us. As we approached the gray modest home that my grandpa and family helped build, the dogs barked with excitement and trailed behind my mom's car. I stepped out of the vehicle and was frequently greeted with warm licks by one of the dogs. They were always happy to see us. My mom told me to hurry up as she walked into Grandma's house. I scurried along and walked into immediate warmth of love and protection. Grandpa was sitting on the couch looking like he was asleep, his head hung low and eyes closed. But as soon as we took a few steps inside, his head would slowly rise, and we received his sincere welcoming eyes. "Good morning," he said as he patted the couch next to him motioning me to sit by him. I told my grandpa good morning and reached over him to give him a big hug. As I cuddled him, I could smell his fragrance, a mixture of laundry detergent, faint scent of sweat and dirt, and that "grandpa smell." I looked up at him and asked him, "Where's Grandma?" Before he answered me, I saw and heard Shimasani fussing in the kitchen. Grandma was usually listening to KHAC on the radio while she tended to cooking breakfast or cleaning up the dishes. "Good morning, Grams," I said to her. She looked at me and smiled with deep kindness. My mom quickly said her hellos and instructed me and my little sister to listen to our grandparents, *masani* and *chei*. She reminded us that she would pick us up later while dropping our things on the couch, and then in the same sentence of hello she said her goodbyes and rushed off to work. We were at Shimasani's house, the home and place where powerful teachings developed my sense of being, my sense of womanhood, my sense of indigeneity.

Shimasani grew up on *Diné bikeyah* (the Navajo lands), a place with stunning and expansive land that is tucked within sacred mountains to the east, south, west, and north. Shimasani was born in 1923, an era when boarding schools for Native youth and children were erasing away Indigenous ways of knowing, and creating generations of Indigenous peoples who would later question their identity, their sense of peoplehood and nationhood, and their sense of belonging. Within the circular walls of a humble home that had no running water or electricity, Shimasani grew into this world with perceptive knowledge to view life in beauty; that is *hózho*, that is resistance. Resistance because there was much devastation happening to Indigenous peoples preceding and during this time, loved ones dying too soon or being forced to far-off places to work or attend school, racist policies impacting the daily lives of our people and many more across what is now called America, and a legacy of land stolen that stripped away the way of life of our people. Resistance does not always have to look a specific way or be enacted in a particular practice. Resistance can be maintaining a consciousness of beauty, like seeing the present and future with a glimmer of hope: *hózho*. Resistance in that form can sometimes be the hardest, especially when violence and social inequalities are attacking your people and so many more. The time of Shimasani's birth was also an era when the federal government reinforced an anti-immigrant law by passing the National Origins Act of 1924, which excluded or included who belongs and does not belong in what is now called America, an irony for many Indigenous peoples because we know that the people who wrote those laws have a lineage of relatives who came to this place as immigrants. The 19th Amendment was also passed, giving women the right to vote in 1920, but the right for Natives to vote did not fully occur until 1962, with Utah being the last state to fully guarantee voting rights for Native people. Then in 1924, when Shimasani was 1 year old, Congress passed the Indian Citizenship Act, a law that made all American Indians citizens of the United States. This was another irony for Indigenous peoples: creating "citizenship" to a place that my grandma's mother, and her mother's mother, and generations back had already known that they were part of and connected to, before settlers arrived and created "citizenship."

My grandma attended the Ganado Mission School, which had started as a day school in 1903 with funding by the Presbyterian National Board of Home Missions and later became a boarding school for many Navajos and the first Native school of nursing (Trennert, 2003). Shimasani told me stories of her time there, such as having to drink castor oil when she spoke *Diné ke'ji* (the Navajo language). It was difficult for me to hear that story as Shimasani explained the disgusting taste and texture in her mouth, and the embarrassment she felt in being ridiculed for speaking the language that she thought in her head, prayed to Creator in, and whispered softly to loved ones. There was much ridicule and assimilative measures happening at the old mission school. Through all of that, Shimasani maintained *Diné* ways and imagined possibilities.

After the dishes were washed and the kitchen was polished, Shimasani sat down in front of the sewing machine. The steady rhythm of the machine accelerated as she placed weight on the foot pedal. I remember standing next to her, watching her steadiness and creative expressions as she worked on her latest quilt. Each quilt was explosive with geometric textiles and patterns, colors that reflected the design and the person who she was going to gift her latest creation to. I stood next to her with curiosity and patience. Soon she would need me to help. "Mandy, can you put this thread through the needle, my eyes are getting tired" or "Mandy, cut these pieces of fabric for me, you always cut straight." Eagerly, I squinted my eyes to ensure that the fine thread squeezed through the tiny hole in the needle. Or I sat on the floor with pieces of vibrant fabric and slowly cut squares, rectangles, and sometimes triangles of thin cotton material. Shimasani was always pleased at my willingness to help her. Little did she know that I was the one who felt lucky to be a part of her work for she was instilling in me the talent and creative imagination of *Diné* female artistry. This was particularly salient given the invisible and dehumanizing societal messages of Indigenous peoples that I would later in life learn to endure. Shimasani had planted in me the contrary, an understanding and knowing that who I am as a *Diné* woman was not based on societal views but an aesthetic reflection of Shimasani.

While being with her, I learned how to crochet. She gave me a needle and ball of yarn and taught me how to hold the yarn between my fingers while also maintaining flexibility with my other hand as the needle wove in and out with each motion. We rested by each other working on our projects while watching the soap opera characters Bo and Hope work through another fight on the popular *Days of Our Lives* show. She worked on a new pillow while I worked on creating a square. After each new row, I showed her my progress. She looked at me and my creation and returned that unforgettable kind smile and gracious nod. I was only 4 years old and Shimasani was already making me feel special, valued, and loved. She saw beauty in my creation. She saw beauty in me. She saw beauty in everything. And she showed me how to see beauty in all things too. bell hooks wrote about her grandmother Baba who taught her "we must learn to see," meaning that all objects have a presence and a spiritual aesthetic. She wrote, "Aesthetics then is more than a philosophy or theory of art and beauty; it is a way of inhabiting space, a particular location, a way of looking and becoming" (hooks, 2009, p. 122). Despite my age and despite how society imposes growth benchmarks on children and adults, Shimasani knew what I was capable of being and becoming. Shimasani was the first teacher to instill creative energy and limitless possibilities. She taught me to see beauty and futurity.

On warm summer days Shimasani took me on long walks. We walked up the hills behind the homestead. The dogs happily followed us as we worked our way through the sagebrush, ant hills, and wild grass. As we ventured on various unseen trails, she told me stories. My grandma had a remarkable and precise memory. She knew details such as the exact year and time of past experiences, contextual challenges occurring of the time, and a sharp wit and understanding of life and its intricacies. She reminded me of hooks's (2009) critique on critical thinking skills as assumed to be only based upon class and educational privilege, whereas Shimasani, like Baba, had "memory [that] stands as a challenge to intellectuals" (p. 132). Shimasani did not have a high school diploma, but she did have infinite intelligence. When I was a young child, she taught me about the power of storytelling. I learned to be patient and listen, not to interrupt and ask questions right away, but to allow the story to flow. She told me stories of when she met Grandpa. She told me about attending the mission school. She told me about when she got sick eating too much ice cream in the city. She told me about how the dogs were barking loud the night before. I followed her footsteps and drank in her stories. She also gave me room to tell stories, allowing my creativity to further blossom as I retold an experience or fantasized and wondered out loud. I heard her giggle or agree by saying *aoo'* (yes), indicating that she was listening and interested in what I had to say. There were also nonverbal gestures that signified connection and acknowledgment. In our story sharing there was a deep recognition of history and our place in history. Experience and knowledge were interwoven with history and presence. Story illuminated aesthetics of the storyteller, the storying, and the story listener. I am reminded of Laura Rendón's (2009) work *Sentipensante Pedagogy,* where she stated, "Ancient epistemology is the first way of knowing, the way of our ancestors, the original way of work" (p. 133). For many Indigenous peoples, oral stories are a pedagogical practice that has sustained us over time. I am here today because of those stories of vulnerability, healing, resistance, and liberation. Shimasani was the first teacher to teach me about the powerful role that story and story sharing has in generating a sense of belonging by seeing ourselves and our ancestors in the world of today, yesterday, and tomorrow.

Then we reached our destination. She proceeded to a juniper tree and carefully took a piece of a branch from the tree. She stood there for a bit in front of the juniper tree. I stood nearby in silence and waited for her to let us know when we were ready. I think the dogs even knew to sit still and wait. Then she brushed the dust resting on her pants and motioned for us to return home. I believe that those pausing moments near the juniper tree were her moments of prayer, giving thanks to creation and Creator. As we walked back home, she explained that she was going to burn the juniper into ash so that she could make *tanaashgiizh* (blue mush) for later. She needed ingredients from the tree to make the delicacy even more delicious, *łikan* (sweet). Shimasani eventually taught me how to pick the spiny, thin green-thread, which also blossomed in the summer. They grew in plenty especially after a good rainy season. Some areas near our home and at Fluted Rock had an array of greenthreads with yellow buds of flowers on their tips swaying as the gentle winds came through. She instruct-ed me to not rush when picking the plants from the ground. The first time we ventured together to gather greenthreads, I remember being gently scolded for yanking them unconsciously from the brown soil. She did not yell at me. In fact, I never remember her raising her voice at me unless I trailed off from the house and she was beckoning me to come home: "Maaaannndddyy!! Time to eat!!!" Rather she simply said, "Don't pull them out so hard. Pay attention to what you are do-ing." She told me to be gentle when uprooting the greenthreads from the ground and avoid taking out all the roots so as to leave the seeds and sprinklings for a new growth, new season. We picked a bundle of these plants and then returned to the house to get them prepared for *dééh* (tea).

Shimasani rinsed the plants off and cleaned off any residue that was clinging to the plants. She took the plants outside to dry in the warmth of the sun by laying them on newspapers that were placed on a table. After the plants were dry, we sat at the table and folded each greenthread into tiny bundles. I saw my grandma give *dééh* away to family, friends, and strangers. If someone was not feeling well, she made hot tea and blue mush from the plants we gathered. If my grandpa worked late in the hot sun outside, she supplied him with re-freshing iced tea from the plants we gathered. Whether it was juniper ash, greenthread, or pinon seeds, Shimasani showed me that our sus-tenance comes from the land. I was taught to respectfully gather these materials with gratitude, prayers, and gentleness. And I also learned the value in taking only what is needed, not being greedy by taking all that was available but leaving some for others. I strive to be like her in many ways by giving to others what I have gathered and learned: teachings of relationality—knowing we are all related; aesthetic un-derstandings of communal benevolence to one another and to the land, plants, and waterways; understanding that for us to survive, we must take care of each other.

Every night when the evening news came on at 5 p.m., Shimasani sat in front of the television and waited for the weather report. Her notebook and pen sat on her lap and a cold Coke was in her right hand. Usually dinner was on the stove or in the oven by this time and many of us sat watching the local news with her and grandpa. Around 5:25 p.m. the weather report came on and Grandma placed her Coke on the floor and opened up her notebook. She listened attentively as the newscaster announced the daily temperature, the sunrise time, the sunset time, and the weekly forecast. Shimasani jotted down those figures in her notebook. For as long as I can remember, it was a habit for Grandma to record the movement of the sun, the climate of the land, and the future outlook of our relationship with the land, sky, and universe. I never asked her why she recorded such things. In a way, I understood my grandmother's relationship to the rhythm of the ecosystem.

For example, when I was nearing 5 years old, I remember when she told me that it would be time for me to begin formal schooling, that I would no longer spend most of the days with her. She told me in relation to the seasons. One afternoon, we were taking our usual stroll in Ganado. The air was getting cooler and the leaves on the trees were turning to shades of yellow, red, and orange. Some leaves were falling off of the trees. She told me that all the leaves will fall off some of the trees like the cottonwood that grew beside the water beds and washes. She explained that new leaves eventually would sprout on the trees. And when the leaves were fully grown, it would be soon time for me to begin primary school. She further explained that the cycle of leaves growing, dying/leaving, and growing again was a part of life and could serve as a way for me to recognize when school days begin and end and begin again. Using the trees and seasons, she taught me to pay attention to the world around us, to be present with the presence, to recognize the rhythm and cycles of life beyond human existence. She planted seeds of knowledge that the trees, skies, and water are living beings with unimaginable wisdom. They can teach us a lot if we pay attention. That is why we must care for them as they care for us. At such a young age, she also described changes, transitions, growth, and phases in relation to the world. I did not want to leave her world, but she reminded me that we were inseparable. We are all related and therefore connected with each other.

One night, I was sitting outside with Shimasani. The nights at *Diné bikeyah* were cool, dark, and comforting. Soft glows of light could be seen from homes scattered around. But the most prevalent light visible was from the stars and moon. We sat in the darkness but could see. That evening, the sky was breathtaking as the moon was just above us and the stars sprinkled extra bright. She told me to look at the moon and notice how it was positioned in the deep black sky. The moon was slender and in a large, wide U position. She said that when the moon is sitting in the universe in that way, it meant that rain was coming soon. Rain, as I have been taught, is a divine blessing gifted to us from Creator. Rain nourishes the greenthreads, the juniper, cottonwood, and pinon trees. Rain fills the washes so that our nonhuman relatives could drink for strength and survival. Rain can wash away our sorrows if we let it. Rain blesses all of us. And the moon tells us when blessings were on the way. She told me that blessings are all around us, just as beauty is all around us. She taught me to see in beauty.

"Elder pedagogies sit with you because they are real, because they are alive, and because they are becoming yours, in your own journey, as you listen into silences, ancestors, beauty, nature, sound, and the spinnings of the Universe. And are moved" (Holmes & González, 2017, p. 215). Shimasani showed me that life was not in a simple dichotomy: good versus bad, traditional versus nontraditional, Native versus non-Native, *Diné* versus *bilagaana* (White people). She was a woman of cultural abundance in understanding that life has contradictions, life has complexities, life has constellations. What she cherished was caring for people, caring for the place we call home, and not wasting time or resources—for all are important. Shimasani exemplified *Diné* matrilineal teachings that were passed down by her mother, her mother's mother, and so on—knowledge that she passed down to my mother and to me; knowledge that I am passing down to my children. As teachers, we all have ancestral knowledges that affirms belonging, love, kinship, and beauty. We must share that with others and allow others to see the beauty that resides in them.

This is a book to inform teachers on ways they can consider, take up, reflect upon, and engage in ways to cultivate their classrooms and students' lives. I purposely shared grandmothers' pedagogies from a *Diné* perspective to remind educators that learning happens outside of the walls of schools and institutions—teachings from grandmothers, our elders. Let's not forget that.

RECOMMENDATIONS FOR EDUCATORS:
LESSONS FROM SHIMASANI

Consider how student success is measured. Often outcomes are measured against White normative standards and curriculum that problematizes and positions Indigenous students as deficient, less than, below average, and so on. Rather, Shimasani taught me to not base my sense of being upon societal views, but to see myself as a reflection of my grandmothers. How might schooling measure student success that is more relevant to their lives and experiences?

Design, cultivate, and imagine possibilities (futurities) that are beautified. My grandmothers reinforced possibilities through affirmations (verbal and nonverbal), guidance (that was nonjudgmental and consistent), and creativity. Get to meaningfully know your students' strengths and gifts and cultivate those skills and knowledges. How might classrooms look when Indigenous (and all) students see the potentiality that they offer the world through your loving encouragement?

Nourish storytelling, story sharing, and storying. Explore the multitudes of storying that moves beyond the typical five-paragraph essay constructions and mechanics. Allow students to share and deeply listen to stories through various ways from written, oral, physical expression/physical walks, and through the arts. How might curriculum look when stories are considered as theories (Brayboy, 2005), deserving of time and respected with an understanding that stories carry knowledges that have been passed down from generations to generations?

Understand the deep relationships between people and land and waterways. Much of my learning occurred outside, in the lands near our home. I learned teachings of survival, belonging, sacredness, respect, relationality, love, and continuation from gathering plants and taking walks with Shimasani. With a deep understanding that schoolings and institutions reside on Indigenous lands, and that our relationships to one another and to the land are critical, how might schools and schooling transform?

REFERENCES

Brayboy, B. (2005). Toward a tribal critical race theory. *The Urban Review*, 37(5), 425–446.

Holmes, A., & González, N. (2017). Finding sustenance: An Indigenous relational pedagogy. In D. Paris & H. S. Alim (Eds.), *Culturally sustaining pedagogies: Teaching and learning for justice in a changing world* (pp. 207–224). Teachers College Press.

hooks, b. (2009). *Belonging: a culture of place*. Routledge.

Paris, D., & Alim, H. S. (Eds.). (2017). *Culturally sustaining pedagogies: Teaching and learning for justice in a changing world*. Teachers College Press.

Rendón, L. (2009). *Sentipensate pedagogy: Educating for wholeness, social justice, and liberation*. Stylus Publishing.

Tachine, A. R. (2017). Grandmothers' pedagogy: Lessons for supporting Native students' attendance at universities. In J. Frawley,. S. Larkin,. & J. A. Smith (Eds.), *Indigenous pathways, transitions, and participation in higher education* (pp. 151–168). Springer.

Trennert, R. A. (2003). Sage Memorial Hospital and the nation's first all-Indian school of nursing. *The Journal of Arizona History*, 44(4), 353–374.

CHAPTER 9

Reclaiming Our Position as the Most Important Educators of Our Native Children

Jameson D. Lopez

My mother is my inspiration and my father is my guide, but both were my teachers and educated me about life. I'm Quechan (pronounced kwat'san) from Fort Yuma, California, born in Phoenix Indian Medical Center and raised in a predominately White neighborhood in north Phoenix. My parents were both educators who worked for a small, underfunded college for Native students. Their positions at the college allowed my parents, sisters, and me to travel to Tribal Nations across the United States to promote higher education. Those travels taught me several life lessons: I learned to be thankful watching tarantulas running through the hot summer nights while trying to sleep on the floor on the Apache reservation. I experienced what it meant to be a proud Native, listening to firsthand stories of Kiowa American Indian Movement activists and their occupation of Wounded Knee. I learned the reality of our hardships while trying to encourage children to stop smoking on the Blackfeet reservation. I learned about our ability to be resilient watching our tribal youth continue to live their lives, after attending a cremation ceremony for a young boy who had committed suicide. I ultimately learned how to sacrifice to those in need, watching my parents take pay cuts and continually give of what little money or food we had. Using finances that were left, my parents raised my sisters and me on the edge of an academically advanced school district relative to where we lived previously in the valley of the sun. Nonetheless, I struggled. Not because the work was too rigorous, but because it was irrelevant. What did the work have to do with my understanding of the world at a young age attending funerals, weddings, sleeping arrangements, and my naive understanding of social injustice?

As I think more about what my parents taught me to be Quechan in the world, among many things those lessons showed me that Natives are patient, Natives don't give into stereotypes, Natives are ferocious when preserving our ceremonies, Natives are funny (because our lives are difficult), Natives take care of our own, and Natives adapt. My favorite teachers were by far my parents, hunters of knowledge but teaching me the meaning of success.

My parents emphasized having decent grades, but it was never overemphasized so as to suggest to me at a young age that success was dependent on grades. There were more important concepts to success. Most evident was the concept of giving back as an outcome of educational success. Paris and Alim (2017) suggest that educational outcomes must be measured according to the values of a student's background. The value of giving back was woven into every fabric of lesson that my parents taught me. Yet, the value of giving back is often overlooked by non-Indigenous researchers as an educational outcome despite the relative abundance of research that indicates giving back is an important factor to education (see Huffman, 2011; Makomenaw, 2014; Reyes, 2019; Shield, 2004; Waterman & Lindley, 2013). In the following stories I offer a few reflections on lessons I learned from my parents that underpin the concept of giving back. The stories offer lessons my parents taught me about being *patient*, overcoming *stereotypes*, honoring *ceremony*, finding *humor*, acknowledging *providers*, and *adapting* to life without losing our sense of identity.

BEING *PATIENT*

I had the darkest skin of any kid in class and mistakenly thought I was African American the first 8 years of my life until the teacher called my house and told my mom, "Just want to let you know, your son is going around telling students he is Black." My mom later sat me down and broke the disappointing news that I was not African American. But there was good news at the end. She told me I was Native American, and I was Quechan. I was eager to hear my mom tell me her stories. She shared stories about why the coyote stole the heart of the Creator and ate it—then subsequently told me why my drunk uncle gave me my Quechan name *Kalataway*, meaning coyote.

She taught me about our cremation ceremony and protocols. I was so proud to be Quechan, and like any good mother, my mom used that to her advantage.

When I was 8 years old, I complained about my dirty laundry to my overworked mother. My mom looked at me and said, "JD, Natives do their own laundry; are you Native?" To which I replied, "Yes." She responded, "Well you better do your own laundry." At that same age, I complained about waiting in 5 a.m. lines for the Indian Health Service dentist clinic to open. Once she got tired of my pleas to go home for sleep, she would ask, "JD, are you Native?" I would reply, "Yes." She would say, "Natives are patient, just wait." So I sat there and watched other Natives see the dentist one by one. As the room was less filled with people, I knew it would be my turn soon. I heard my name, and after having a cavity drilled on, I learned patience was not such a bad thing after all. However, I took those things to heart. If my mom told me Natives were patient or do their own laundry, and Quechan are Natives, then I must be patient, and I must do my own laundry. In my later years, I realized those beginning lessons of patience were important to giving back, because you don't see the benefit of your labor as soon as it happens.

My mom was often tired from working constantly as a faculty member in the Elementary Education Department and tired from raising my sisters and me. Nonetheless, during her time as an instructor, she trained hundreds of Native American teachers. However, it was not all at once. It was a handful of students each year during the course of 22 years. She taught me that giving back takes patience, but the results can be remarkable.

OVERCOMING *STEREOTYPES*

In kindergarten, I had an amazingly brilliant teacher who acted stupid on Columbus Day and Thanksgiving. She dressed us up like Pilgrims and fake Native Americans on those days. I'm sure some of you remember because it still happens to this day. You get some construction paper, glue, and start making your costumes. Everyone wanted to be Native, because the crafts looked better. Plus, society romanticizes Natives so much as being warriors and running barefoot with the wind that it made the idea of being Native awesome. And let's face it, Pilgrims historically sucked. Being a Pilgrim in class only involved black and white paper and making a nun-type hat to put on your head. But if you were a fake Native in class, you got all the colorful construction paper for feathers, and got the foil to make all your silver turquoise bling.

Well, only half the class could be Native, and half could be Pilgrims. And for that day, everyone wanted to be Native. Only problem was, it was done by lottery: You picked a race from a hat. And I remember thinking, I can't wait to be a Native. I still did not quite understand that I was Native, but I knew better than to want to be a Pilgrim. Like what were they known for, other than being diseased?

It was my turn to pick from the hat, and as I was praying to be a Native for the day, the Creator played a joke on me. That brilliant ignorant teacher said, "You get to be a Pilgrim." Like what the . . . I'm a Pilgrim. I sat there all mad, the only Brown kid making a black-and-white hat and felt inferior to the fake Natives in the class. And all I can think now is, "The one day when everyone wanted to be Native was the day I didn't get to be one."

I later told my Dad about the event, but he told me to simply prove them wrong. He paid less attention to what people said, but rather focused his energy into action. He started his college administration position as the dean of students in the early 1980s and was given a different title than the previous dean, because the board of regents did not want the title of "Dean," to go to his head. The board of regents believed that Natives were incapable of having the experience to fill the position. Rather than giving into what people with positional authority said, he always believed in doing the work. It was a lesson to me that sometimes the best way to disprove stereotypes is to show people who we are through action. As opposed to telling people we don't dress in construction-paper headdresses and live in teepees, we need to do work that shows who we are.

HONORING *CEREMONY*

Besides the need to look presentable, there are two reasons that my mom cut my hair as a kid: (1) lice, and (2) funerals. Lice were straightforward. Lice got out of hand and sometimes rather than going through my hair with a fine-tooth comb strand by strand, my mom cut my hair.

Funerals were a little different. I can't remember the first funeral I went to (my parents took us to a lot of funerals as kids because my Dad was a licensed minister). But I remember bits and pieces of the first time I went to our Big House. And if I am honest with myself about the first time I went, it was a bit scary . . . because I did not understand it.

As we approached the Big House, where our tribe holds our wakes, you could hear the singers' gourds and see women start to sway to the rhythm of our ancient songs through the small window openings. I walked in and saw the old wooden pews beneath the dim lighting and the mourning family with women crying at the open casket. My mom directed me to go shake hands with the family members mourning, and then we went to sit down. We just sat there, no talking, some whispering, and a lot of reflecting. I watched the Bird and Pipa singers most of the night, and watched the Quechan women stand and sit during the songs. After we had spent a few hours there, my mom said we were leaving. We proceeded to shake hands again, but this time with everyone in the Big House. We squeezed through the small aisles to shake everyone's hand, and I watched as my mom smiled at some of her family and childhood friends. Before we left, I went with my parents next door to eat some pasole and tortillas and watched them visit with our relatives and friends they hadn't seen in years.

I went to my nana's house to sleep for a few hours, and the next morning my parents woke me up to bring me to the cremation ceremony. I watched as my uncles brought the body out of the casket and laid it between the cottonwood trees. Soon after, they asked for blankets and then my uncle stood there and said a word in Quechan meaning clothes. My mom leaned toward me and said, "Take your shirt off." I did not understand why, but I also did not question her. As I started to see everyone putting their shirts and dresses on top of the body with the blankets, I took my shirt off and put it in too. My uncles lit it all on fire. I stood there watching the remains, blankets, and clothes become engulfed in flames with smoke leading to the morning sky. We left the ceremony not too long after, and that evening my mom cut my hair.

I never quite understood the tradition of why we threw our clothes into the fire, but a few weeks ago I was sitting with an elder. Among the many things he imparted to me, he mentioned that during the death of the Creator in our tribe's creation story the animals did not know how to mourn, so they began to take their ears and tails off to throw into the fire. A piece of us dies when someone we love passes away, and it is one way we remember that. In a similar vein, it is why my mom cut my hair, to signify a piece of me was taken and a piece of me was given. Taking the time to participate in our ceremonies is how we let people know who we are, a lesson I took from my mom and dad.

FINDING *HUMOR*

I was mischievous most of my childhood, but it also meant I was entertaining for my parents. I was conducting my nightly routine a 6-year-old goes through. Mostly messing around, asking for water, using the bathroom a lot. All that to try to stay up for a few extra minutes. We were living at the 6th drive in Phoenix, Arizona. I was wearing an old, oversized T-shirt going on my fourth or fifth trip to the bathroom. This time, not that it was not there all the other times, I saw an orange and white Bic disposable safety razor sitting next to the sink. The same one I watched my dad use in the morning. My dad could grow a full beard, something I still can't do at age 33.

But I saw the razor and thought I would try it on the only facial hair I had in those moments. My eyebrows. I took the safety razor and guided it along the left side of my left eyebrow. I looked in the mirror afterward and thought to myself, "It did not work." I put it back on the counter and walked out of the bathroom. I nonchalantly walked back into the living room to wait until my parents told me to go to bed for the fourth or fifth time. But instead I was greeted with my mom's puzzled look and question, "Did you shave your eyebrow?" To which I replied, "I don't know." My mom insisted, "Did you use that razor?" I said, "Sure." She continued, "Well, I think you shaved it." She and my dad both laughed and told me to go back to bed. It's the reason my left eyebrow still grows a little differently than my right. And then I witnessed it at a camp I was working at on the Nez Perce reservation about 14 years ago.

I was in Lapwai, Idaho, working at a Native youth camp. As with all kids, there was one Native kid who was particularly rowdy. He was continually sneaking away, disrupting the instructors, and just being generally mischievous. He was assigned to my team and shadowed me most of the week. And as rowdy as this kid was, he was equally hilarious. As we were gathering for the morning activities, I saw him stroll by, and I said, "Hey, did you shave your eyebrows?" He started laughing and said, "Yeah." I mean, it was obvious, people look funny with no eyebrows. And I just laughed. The rest of the week he used a sharpie to draw in his eyebrows. When he was angry, he would draw his eyebrows with a gradual slope and quick drop at the end. When he was happy, he made them little hills.

My point is, if you don't think you're funny or you want to be funnier or if you want to be more entertaining, shave your eyebrows.

Giving humor to the world is never a mistake, and it's needed to cope and live through the hardships that we face as Native people.

ACKNOWLEDGING *PROVIDERS*

One Christmas Eve when I was around 8 years old, I asked my mom if Jesus and Santa were friends, and she said, "Yes, they are close friends." That night I was going to bed, and my sister Camie saw me and said, "JD, Santa is not real." The rest of that night we spent sneaking in the hallway watching my parents and older sister Joy wrap our presents. It wasn't at all traumatizing, but I have often wondered how I would handle the Santa myth with my kids.

I have two kids, and I'm not all that excited about them believing in Santa—partly because I don't want them sitting on Santa's lap because (1) you have to pay money to do it, and (2) I do not like the idea of the kids sitting on some old White dude's lap who asks them, "What can I get you for Christmas?" We do not need to reinforce that "White-savior mentality" (i.e., a brilliant White person comes and saves the poor, needy minorities, who earnestly need saving). But I need my kids to know that Brown faces gave them these presents, just like I had a Brown face who brought me presents when I was little. We did not have White Santa, we had Brown Santa, and sure, he may have been drinking a little.

Nonetheless, before I knew Santa was fake, we had drunk Santa. I think every family occasionally had a drunk family member, and one of ours came at Christmas time reincarnated as drunk Santa. I actually never knew which family member was drunk Santa . . . my cousins probably would, but I was too little to really remember. I thought he was for-real Santa. But I remember every Christmas we had a gathering at my nana's house on Christmas Eve, and my nana would make us wait until midnight for Santa to bring presents. Santa would come and bring us presents, but he never came on time. So around 1:30 a.m., throughout my childhood, we would meet Santa. He would stumble out of his sleigh and walk toward the house. I would be jumping around because I was happy to finally be opening presents. He was always a character. One year he fell out of a lawn chair, and in his slurred words, he would ask us, "What do you want?" And coming from a Christian home and not ever really smelling alcohol ever in my life, I always knew something was weird. But I would go with it. And I would take my turn going to sit on Santa's lap. Let's be clear, this Santa never brought what we wanted. These Christmases were really about family. Normally Santa, or my nana, would buy us stuff like tube socks or soap on a rope. Not complaining, but all those years Santa never brought us our heart's desire. It was our parents who brought us our presents. Making me learn at an early age, that it wasn't White people who will give us what we need in progress, it will always be our own people, Native people who can give back.

ADAPTING TO LIFE

"Rez ball" is somewhat of a lawless form of basketball often played on dirt courts with plywood backboards, using a ball covered in bull-heads that barely bounces. There is usually not an out-of-bounds, or three-point line, and painfully there are normally no fouls. If you ever played rez ball, you would understand what I mean.

I was in northern Arizona one time, at a camp meeting. My dad was speaking, and I was out playing ball during the day. I lost track of time, and before I knew it people started coming out of the service. I kept playing ball, and soon some of the adults started joining. There weren't any rules, and we were just more or less shooting around. As the shooting progressed, we became more and more competitive, not really playing any particular game—just rez ball. One of the older, bigger gentlemen got the ball. I ran up to him, punched him in the stomach, and said, "Give me the ball, fat boy." I was 7 or 8, and he was in college. My dad popped up out of nowhere. He took me around back and whooped me. Needless to say, I wasn't allowed to play rez ball.

Sometime this past year my dad and I were talking. In my later years of life, we've become philosophical in our conversations, contemplating life, identity, ceremonies, and so on. He brought up to me about playing rez ball. He said, "Remember playing rez ball, and eventually you started playing on that club team?" I said, "Yeah, I remember." My dad went on, "You can't play rez ball the rest of your life, eventually you gotta learn the rules of the game if you want to move to the next level."

We literally applied that concept to different things in our life. I applied it to the thought of going from high school to college. We mentioned it in regard to nonprofit organizations. Eventually, we need to learn the rules if we're going to play at another level. I was lucky to have a dad who put people in my path who knew rules to different games. Whether it was fixing doorknobs, laying flagstone, getting into graduate school, and so on. It's hard as parents to know that we don't have all the answers for our kids, but I'm glad that I have family and friends who can help me along the way. The ability to adapt will always help the next generation of Natives enter into new spaces. It makes me happy to know that my own kids (Luna and Gordie) won't be stuck just playing rez ball the rest of their life. I'll have the chance to teach them to play the game by different rules and move between spaces and bring people into their lives who will help them as well.

CONCLUSION

These few lessons from my parents (who were teachers to me) underpinned my understanding of giving back, a concept important to my understanding of educational success rooted in who I am as Quechan. The concept of giving back my parents taught me was through learning about being patient, overcoming stereotypes, honoring ceremony, finding humor, acknowledging providers, and adapting to life without losing our sense of identity. Giving back is often overlooked by non-Indigenous teachers as an educational outcome, but Indigenous teachers documented the role of giving back as being instrumental to our educational success as Native people. The concept of giving back is rooted in more Indigenous knowledge, whereas many tribes subscribe that reciprocity is important to our culture. Preservice and inservice teachers should seek to understand the role of giving back using deep concepts of Indigenous ways of knowing and being. We should seek to answer questions, such as how can giving back be incorporated in the P–12 classroom in ways that validate traditional Indigenous knowledge? For example, one concept that may encompass the concept of giving back is the "warrior spirit." For Quechan, the warrior spirit is Kwaname. Introducing Indigenous knowledge such as Kwaname into the classroom gives Quechan and other Natives alike a chance to reclaim how we are defining educational success and reclaim our position as the most important teachers of our Native children.

Recommendations

1. Preservice and inservice teachers should seek to understand and be able to describe the complexities of Indigenous knowledge.

2. Preservice and inservice teachers should seek to understand the role of giving back as an educational outcome.

3. Preservice and inservice teachers should seek to critically engage in discussions around how to teach students within the context of the surrounding tribal communities that privileges the tribal community notions of being and knowing.

REFERENCES

Huffman, T. E. (2011). Plans to live on a reservation following college among American Indian students: An examination of transculturation theory. *Journal of Research in Rural Education, 26*(3), 1–13.

Makomenaw, M. (2014). Goals, family, and community: What drives tribal college transfer student success. *Journal of Student Affairs Research and Practice, 51*(4), 380–391.

Paris, D., & Alim, H. S. (Eds.). (2017). *Culturally sustaining pedagogies: Teaching and learning for justice in a changing world.* Teachers College Press.

Reyes, N. A. (2019). "What am I doing to be a good ancestor?" An Indigenized phenomenology of giving back among Native college graduates. *American Educational Research Journal, 56*(3), 603–637.

Shield, R. W. (2004). The retention of Indigenous students in higher education: Historical issues, federal policy, and Indigenous resilience. *Journal of College Student Retention: Research, Theory & Practice, 6*(1), 111–127.

Waterman, S. J., & Lindley, L. S. (2013). Cultural strengths to persevere: Native American women in higher education. *NASPA Journal About Women in Higher Education, 6*(2), 139–165.

CHAPTER 10

Honoring My (Academic) Matriarchs

Theresa Stewart-Ambo

Reminiscing on my academic journey to date, as this journey is far from over, I recognize that no person walks this road alone. Now an assistant professor at the University of California (UC)–San Diego, I spend much of my time independently thinking and writing. The journey can be lonely, but I constantly remind myself that I am not alone. Staring out the window while tethered to a desk, I often reflect on *all* the individuals that have supported this process: those who walk before, alongside, and behind me. Over the years, many people selflessly loved and guided me when it was most needed, especially Indigenous women. They steered me when I wandered aimlessly, and picked me up and lent me their strength when I lacked the courage to stand on my own. This chapter honors those women: the women who have guided and nurtured my educational pursuits.

My research resists the legacy of colonial education—a system that my ancestors, relatives, peers, and I continue to endure. My scholarship specifically focuses on the relationship between public postsecondary institutions in California and local American Indian nations to challenge practices and assumptions of relationality, responsibility, and reciprocity (i.e., accountability). Along the way, I have also challenged Western conceptions of love, care, and self-care in my writing to illuminate how Indigenous people in academia draw on ancestral knowledges and practices as they navigate assimilative and outright hostile institutions. I add to these writings here to mark the role of love and bravery embodied by Indigenous women and women of color on educational pathways. bell hooks's (2000) elaboration on love as a verb is how I operationalize this term, which is often conflated with feelings. Drawing from the work of Erich Fromm, hooks defines *love* as "the will to extend one's self for the purpose of nurturing one's own and another's spiritual growth" (p. 4). Likewise, *bravery* is "courageous behavior or character." To this end, this writing reflects the ways in which these women enact love and bravery through their actions, existence, resilience, success, and advocacy.

In the following, I write about my ancestors, some of whom I never met but whose blood courses through my veins, allowing me to feel their daily presence in my life. I write about my great-great-grandmother, great grandmother, and grandmother who inspired my work in Indigenous education. I write, albeit briefly, about my mother, aunties, sisters, sister scholars, colleagues, and friends who shaped the way I navigate the academy. Lastly, I write about two mentors, Sylvia Hurtado and Mishuana Goeman, to highlight the ways effective professors (as teachers) operate as windows and mirrors to Indigenous students. Each woman represents a mirror or window—that is, a cultural reflection or opening to opportunities. May these stories impress upon preservice and inservice teachers the importance of intergenerational and multiracial relationships with the living and deceased when serving students, particularly Indigenous students.

CALLING ON MY MATRILINEAL LINE

Matrilineality and matriarchy are not one and the same. Barker (2017) points out that *matrilineality* indicates biological relationships, thus "not necessarily indicative of matriarchy" (p. 13). A *matriarch* is "a woman who is the head of a family or tribe" or "an older woman who is powerful within a family or organization." Thus, a *matriarchy* is "a system of society or government ruled by a woman or women." These definitions only minimally describe Indigenous understandings of matriarchy. I begin by calling on this line of women by acknowledging my ancestors and relatives, the matriarchy that made me, the lineage that courses through my veins, whose every sacrifice and decision brought me to my current place in life.

Maria Francisca Lisalde—my great-great-grandmother—was born in 1852, 3 years after California was brought under U.S. authority, when the country and state were aggressively removing American Indians from their homelands. In 1850 California had passed the Act for the Government and Protection of Indians, which legalized the indentured servitude (i.e., slavery) of all California Indians. The federal and state governments also conspired—although rather publicly—in funding militia to conduct expeditions of extermination against California Indians. Francisca was born at Pio Pico's house in Los Angeles, eventually making her way to San Timoteo. She married Loretto Gonzales of Santa Ysabel, and together they raised eight children (Joseph, George, Emanuel, Paul, Nina, Ramona, Louis, and Narcisa Gonzales). Known in the region for her doctoring, Francisca was knowledgeable about the medicinal properties of native plants and served as a midwife. Her grandchildren—my great aunties and uncles—remarked on the many times she cured their illnesses. The sociopolitical tensions made it criminal to identify as California Indian. While I never knew Francisca, I imagine the tenacity required to survive this violent time. Francisca reflects the strength and resilience of my bloodlines.

Ramona (Ballesteros) Gonzales—my great-grandmother—was born in 1896 in Arizona. She lived during the time when American Indians were denied U.S. citizenship and considered "wards of the state," federal Indian boarding schools were forcibly removing children from their homes, and the Dawes Allotment Act (1887) was dividing up Indian lands for individual ownership. At the age of 15, Ramona moved from Tempe, Arizona, to San Bernardino, California, with her sister and toddler sons (Leonard and Gilbert) to escape her abusive father. A single mother, she found work in the downtown area of San Bernardino where she met Louis Florian Gonzales. They married and had eight children (Raymond, Dora, Emma, Carmelita, Carlos, Louis George, Cora, and Mary Jeanette). Together they raised their children with the aid of Francisca in San Timoteo. Ramona and Louis sent their children to Saint Boniface Indian Industrial School, the same school Louis had attended. Before sending their daughters to Saint Boniface, my grandmother told me that Ramona cut her and Emma's hair, telling them that she didn't want the teachers to cut her daughters' hair. Like Francisca, Ramona's bravery, too, reflects the tenacity necessary to endure and survive.

Carmelita (Gonzales) Aguila—my grandmother—was born in 1922 in San Timoteo Canyon. Like her grandmother and mother, Carmen (i.e., Carmelita) was not born a citizen of the United States (the American Indian Citizenship Act was not passed until 1924, 2 years following her birth). At the age of 5, Carmen was taken to Saint Boniface Indian Industrial School in Banning, California, along with five of her siblings. She attended Saint Boniface until 7th grade, when she ran away and never returned. At home, newly arriving Mormon ranchers cut off water to their family ranch, forcing them into the city of Redlands. Carmen is my earliest memory of our family's matriarch. She was the first person to receive me after I was born. I took the name Theresa, the name of her first daughter, a child she lost shortly after birth. Carmen affectionately doted on me throughout her life, repeating my birth story and protectively claiming that I belonged to her. Our special relationship did not stop there. When I attended college, she penned me several letters the first few years. My journey through academia started with trying to understand the parts of her life that she concealed from us to protect us (and herself). In these ways, Carmen was a window: guiding me to my work in education and American Indian studies. Learning about her life opened the window to knowing myself, while simultaneously opening a window into my career. Even though she has left this world, I know that she continues to walk with me, guiding me in my work.

Dolores Maria (Aguila) Stewart—my mother—was born June 27, 1958, to Carmen and Calistro Aguila. A child of the 1960s and teen of the 1970s, Dolores grew up during the civil rights movement. As part of the American Indian Self-Determination and Educational Assistance Act of 1970, she secured summer jobs through the workforce program at a local San Bernardino Indian center, one of which included bagging lunches in local elementary schools. I have always been close with my mother. Growing up, I worked with my mother in the yard and kitchen. Inarguably, my mother—and father—were my first teachers. Our bond was solidified when I was enrolled in my Master of Education program, when I visited my parents nearly every Friday for breakfast. Sitting at our oval kitchen table flanked with a tablecloth, my mother and I sipped copious amounts of coffee and recapped each week. We never shied away from difficult conversations about racism, sexism, power, and privilege, and intensely revisited stories from our lives. My most vivid memories are of watching my mother—a regal 5-foot woman of color—confronting my often-self-righteous schoolteachers and principals, the local department store managers and cashiers, and restaurant staff. At the time, I was embarrassed by my mother's boldness and bravery. I now recognize that these characteristics are necessary for being an academic, as we are required to conceptualize innovative research and share it with the world for criticism. Never afraid to speak her mind and intolerant of disrespect, my mother's bravery serves as a mirror of how I must navigate academia.

There are many other women to mention—aunties, cousins, sisters, colleagues, and peers. My aunties showed me how to laugh, work hard, and be unconditionally loving. While raising their children, they each confronted alcoholism, physical and emotional abuse, and poverty. Along the way, they could have hardened their hearts, pushed everyone away, and shut the world out. Instead, they remained soft, loving, kind, and generous women. My favorite memories are laughing with my aunts, telling dirty jokes, shopping at thrift stores, going to local Indian casinos to gamble and eat, and making cookies every Christmas season. Now we talk and text regularly. They are the first to affirm and encourage any one of my social media posts. Each in their own way, they are mirrors to the strong Indigenous woman I desire to be.

Among these relatives are my sisters (Ramona and Kelly), two diametrically different women. Ramona (named after our great-grandma) has a strong silence—always watching and listening. She has always been on the other end of the phone, soaking up my tears and listening to my worries. Kelly, on the other hand, is loquacious, speaking a mile a minute, multidirectionally. She has a sponge for a brain (that I have yet to see be saturated), absorbing the most microscopic pieces of knowledge. Kelly and I have a bond through our individual and collective academic journeys and research. My sisters are mirrors, reflecting back to me who I am and can be. At the same time, they sacrificially (and quite literally) held open windows for me to crawl through so that I can enter spaces they have and might never traverse.

I would be remiss if I did not acknowledge the generations of Indian women who have befriended and mentored me. Although there are simply too many to list them all, Robin, Dianna, Sunshine, Virginia, and Katya went to school with me and remain my closest friends. Years and life changes later, we talk, text, and visit regularly. Our lives have taken us in drastically different directions, but we are still bonded. Likewise, on my professional journey at UCLA, I crossed paths with other Indian women. Together we held the front line, enduring the racism and sexism entrenched within institutions. Over the years, my relationships with these women have changed. We've moved from seeing or messaging each other daily to very sporadic interactions, transitioned from colleagues to friends and mentors to colleagues, and stopped sharing a physical space with each other. Navigating the changes to these relationships has not been easy, particularly for me, but I cherish the journey we had together.

CALLING ON MY (ACADEMIC) MATRIARCHS

Throughout my K–12 public education it was not safe to openly identify as Luiseno and Tongva. La Puente, California—the city where I
grew up—is located within my Tongva homelands. Throughout my
upbringing, I learned of city lore that situated my hometown on top
of an "ancient Indian village." To honor this history, the high school
adopted an Indian mascot with stereotypical Plains Indian imagery.
Football games included cheerleaders decked out in faux headdresses
leading the audience in tomahawk hand-chops to the beat of the
marching band drums. Dances convened at the "wigwam." It was not
a safe environment, so I intentionally withheld this identity from my
peers and teachers. While home reflected one identity, school reflected
otherwise, and my teachers did not need to be supportive of my cultural identity. Of course, I did have some incredible teachers. Ms. Guz-
man offered me my first job in the field of education: calling parents in
the summer to schedule counseling sessions. Mr. Slakey took a small
group of us to the Ukraine for a 1-month National Science Foundation
cultural exchange, providing me my first international experience. After sharing that I had no plans to attend college, Mr. Ronquillo inter-
vened with SAT, ACT, and college waivers. These teachers certainly
served as windows to opportunities that I never would have imagined
for myself as a first-generation college student from a working-class
family living in an industrial city.

This chapter calls on me to reflect on teachers that did, in fact,
have an impactful role and served as either a mirror or opened a window to other opportunities. Leaning on *culturally relevant/sustaining/
responsive pedagogy* literature helps me understand how it was not
until college, and much later into this journey, that teachers (in this
case professors) served as windows to my professional aspirations and
mirrors that reinforced my indigeneity. Ladson-Billings (1995) argues
that *culturally relevant pedagogies* "help students to accept and affirm
their cultural identity while developing critical perspectives that challenge inequities that schools (and other institutions) perpetuate."
Building on this, Paris (2012) and Paris and Alim (2017) argue that
culturally sustaining pedagogies "seek to perpetuate and foster—to sustain—linguistic, literate, and cultural pluralism as part of schooling for
positive social transformations" (Paris & Alim, 2017, p. 1). Castagno
and Brayboy (2008) write about *culturally responsive schooling* to say
that teachers must possess a set of dispositions, attitudes, values, and

knowledges to be successful with Indigenous students—being caring, holding students to high expectations, and valuing tribal communities and cultures (Castagno & Brayboy, 2008, p. 969).

In the next section, I give specific focus to two professors, mentors, and now colleagues, Sylvia Hurtado and Mishuana Goeman, who have illuminated (and continue to illuminate) through their actions (often unintentionally) the ways that love and bravery operate in academia. I narrate encounters with Sylvia and Mishuana from my doctoral experience that served as turning points in my academic trajectory. These moments are intimately tied to culturally sustaining pedagogies, highlighting the ways that love and bravery fortify the presence and practice of Indigenous epistemologies and anti-colonial praxis in academia.

Sylvia Hurtado is a professor at UCLA's Graduate School of Education and Information Studies. She is a scholar on higher education, most known for her contributions on campus racial climate. My first encounter with Sylvia was in fall 2012, when I was enrolled in the Master of Education in Student Affairs program and taking her course Fundamentals of US Higher Education Systems. I intentionally enrolled in Sylvia's section, because, at the time, I needed to take a class with a woman of color, see how she taught, and hear her perspectives on higher education. Little did I know that this class would ignite in me the passion to pursue a PhD. As expected, I was the only Indigenous student in the course and found myself making contributions to include this perspective. I met with Sylvia and the teaching assistant (Gina Garcia) about my interest in American Indian educational issues, and they were always encouraging. At the end of November, I approached Sylvia to discuss applying to the PhD in Higher Education program. I was late to the meeting—running on Indian time—but she patiently waited for me for an hour. Sitting in the UCLA Faculty Center, I told her that I was thinking of applying and asked if I was "insane" for thinking myself capable of such a pursuit. Sylvia enthusiastically indicated that I would be a great fit—that my critical thinking was developing, my writing was clear and strong, and interest in American Indians was needed. She offered to write my letter of recommendation on the spot; mind you, as a first-generation college student I knew little about admission procedures at that point in my career.

Months later, after I started the program, Sylvia offered me my "first official research opportunity," inviting me to participate in a

campus climate study at Cornell University. At the time, I was looking for full-time jobs, applied, and was interviewing. Sylvia advised
against it. After I avoided her emails, she chased me down the hallway after convocation, very directly got after me for not responding,
and invited me to join the research team. The Cornell study became
an entry point to a graduate student research position at the Higher
Education Research Institute, but more importantly it was my introduction to campus climate research. Over the years, I continued this
research with Sylvia (and Adriana Ruiz-Alvarado) working on grants,
retention-related studies, and conducting a 2-year study for a private
foundation on low-income students. I struggled with every project
because they never explicitly focused on American Indians, but Sylvia
never let up. It was a tough type of love.

There are many things that I remember so clearly about working
with Sylvia—her questioning glances over a small pair of eyeglasses,
her early morning emails. I loved to witness her confidence. She was
only about 5 feet tall, and I rejoiced in watching her walk into any
room and take down the sturdiest person with a single laugh. And
it continues to bring me joy to see her beam with pride with every
advisee's accomplishment—from dissertation proposal to defense,
postdoctoral fellowship award to tenure-track job offer. Sylvia became
an example of how faculty of color can be in support of Indigenous
students—opening window after window for me to hop through. She
has even pushed me through them on occasion when I clearly feared
what was on the other side. At every turn, Sylvia saw my potential.
She always knew what I needed, when I didn't know it myself. She
supported and encouraged me, was patient, embraced my rebellious-
ness (likely because she saw some of herself in me at times). There
are many ways in which Sylvia was also a mirror, reflecting back to
me the ability to retaining passion and integrity on an educational
journey.

Mishuana Goeman is a UCLA professor of Gender Studies, current
chair of the American Indian Studies interdepartmental program, and
first Special Advisor to the Chancellor of Native American and Indigenous Affairs. She is a scholar of Indigenous feminisms and spatial and temporal (re)mapping. I met Mishuana in 2009, when she
came to UCLA. At the time, I was a full-time Student Affairs professional staff member and we did not have much interaction. But my
first recollection of Mishuana was earlier, when I was a doctoral student and she guest-lectured in an American Indian Studies/Sociology

course for which I was a TA. Wearing a purple dress, she sashayed into class, fumbled with the computer and projector, and gave a lecture on Haudenosaunee Sky Woman. While I had taken classes from other Indigenous women at UCLA, I was not at the place where their actions resonated with me. Watching Mishuana in this moment was a serious turning point for me, which I credit for being the moment I decided to pursue the professoriate. For the first time ever, I saw the possibility of being an Indigenous faculty who is successful in working with and researching one's own community.

In 2016, Mishuana invited me to contribute a story map to the Mapping Indigenous Los Angeles (MILA) website. MILA is a digital space mapping the temporal and spatial geographies of indigeneity in Los Angeles, for which I contributed a map on Indigenous education. Through this work, Mishuana not only uplifted me as an Indigenous scholar through an anti-colonial praxis by providing opportunities (i.e., windows), but also helped me resist settler narratives of erasure and colonization through a remapping of special terrain. This project also demonstrated possibilities for community-engaged research and projects.

In October of 2016, my interest grew to apply for the University of California President's Postdoctoral Fellowship Program. I received emails throughout the summer and had a serious desire to extend my research timeline. Because she had held the fellowship previously, I reached out to Mishuana for advice. She made time to meet over coffee. Sitting in Luvall Commons, she talked about her experience on fellowship and offered encouraging words. Months later we sat down again in her office and poured over my statements. I knew she didn't really have the time, that I wasn't her student, but she made space for me in her schedule. Telling me where to tweak the statement, Mishuana helped conceptually connect my personal and research statements. A few months later, I was successfully awarded one of 15 fellowships from a pool of nearly 1,000 applicants.

I moved to UC–San Diego after graduation and completed the 2-year fellowship. When I started to search for a tenure-track faculty position in education, Mishuana was there again, advising me on the negotiation process. I leaned on her, and several others, for advice on how to place value on myself and my scholarship. On a phone call Mishuana very poignantly told me, "What you negotiate is not about you, but about the work that Indigenous women did before you and the value placed on Indigenous women after you." I wrote these words on a Post-it Note and placed it at the front of my desk as a constant reminder. Hearing these words, I was reminded of my place in this matriarchy of Indigenous women and women of color: This journey was not about salary negotiations but much more about honoring our predecessors and creating a legacy for those who follow.

There are many things I fondly remember about Mishuana over the course of our work together (work that has not ended). Of course, there is her wild and curly hair, but more so it is the responsibility of Indigenous people to support and provide opportunities to each other to grow personally and intellectually. While Mishuana provided me with countless opportunities or windows, she was and continues to be a mirror.

CONCLUSION

Here I draw out recommendations to preservice and inservice teachers who desire to leave impactful and lasting impressions on their students. I first point to the importance of ancestral and intergenerational relationships with the deceased and living on educational journeys. As Indigenous people, we are not far removed from our relationships with our ancestors or relatives, holding close to familial sacrifice and drawing on ancestral strength and wisdom to navigate foreign places. Teachers must account for intergenerational relationships—inviting these relationships into pedagogy and the classrooms and seeking ways to support Indigenous students.

Moreover, is it important to acknowledge the limited number of Indigenous elementary and secondary teachers serving Indigenous students; resulting in the rare occurrence of Indigenous teachers serving Indigenous students. Culturally relevant pedagogies move us "to perpetuate and foster—to sustain—linguistic, literate, and cultural pluralism as part of schooling for positive social transformations" (Paris & Alim, 2017, p. 1). As such, non-Indigenous teachers *must* be hyper-aware of their responsibility and roles in supporting Indigenous students and communities as cultural sustainability. Many lessons can be gleaned from my experiences for teachers: providing counsel, presenting opportunities, offering resources, affirming and validating knowledge and experience, and making learning culturally relevant. Teachers must also see the potential when and where students and families have not been taught to observe academic possibilities.

To close, I circle back to the role of bravery and love embodied and espoused by these women on my academic journey—not only for me but for other students. In many instances, their actions were necessary to survive the world and academia. Likewise, they courageously demonstrated love to me (and other students) through counsel, guidance, time, written and verbal feedback, and affirmations that allowed for my academic and professional growth. For me, these acts highlight the ways in which Indigenous epistemologies and anti-colonial praxis continue to exist in schools and education.

REFERENCES

Barker, J. (Ed.). (2017). *Critically sovereign: Indigenous gender, sexuality, and feminist studies*. Duke University Press.

Castagno, A., & Brayboy, B. (2008). Culturally responsive schooling for Indigenous youth: A review of the literature. *Review of Educational Research, 78*(4), 941–993.

hooks, b. (2000). *All about love: New visions*. HarperCollins.

Ladson-Billings, G. (1995). Toward a theory of culturally relevant pedagogy. *American Educational Research Journal, 32*(3), 465–491.

Paris, D. (2012). Culturally sustaining pedagogy: A needed change in stance, terminology, and practice. *Educational researcher, 41*(3), 93–97.

Paris, D., & Alim, H. S. (Eds.). (2017). *Culturally sustaining pedagogies: Teaching and learning for justice in a changing world*. Teachers College Press.

Part IV

LATINX PERSPECTIVES

The Latinization of Education

CHAPTER 11

Cultural Affirmations of Giftedness

An Autoethnography of My Experiences with Educational Leadership Faculty at an HBCU

Lisa Maria Grillo

As early as age 3, my Black American mother referred to me as brilliant. When I completed a task that she deemed advanced for my age, she would look at me and plainly state, "You have a brilliant mind, Lisa." I recall her gaze as she uttered the words. She was devoid of pride or admiration. In no way did it appear that she saw my intelligence as a reflection of her own intelligence or mothering. Instead, she was filled with expectation, as if to convey a deep sense of responsibility accompanying this God-given gift. My mother, a woman in love with everyone and everything Black, believed that I was obligated to use this gift toward the upliftment of Black people. She was very clear about this.

My mother knew quite a bit about the politics of race, culture, and intelligence. A special educator with over 30 years of experience, my mother began her professional career as a teacher of students with intellectual disabilities (then called students with mental retardation) in Southern California, teaching children of Mexican migrant workers. My mother would often express frustration that the children were misidentified as disabled due to their lack of English proficiency. She felt the school district had failed them.

My Afro-Cuban father, on the other hand, never verbally addressed my intelligence. Yet, I knew he believed strongly in it. Throughout my childhood, he showed disappointment with any grade lower than an A on my grade reports. "You're not good, you're excellent," he would state, referring to the grade report's legend defining the grade of B as

125

"good." Perhaps the strongest indicator of my father's perception of me was the way in which he engaged me in conversations. He never lowered his style of speech by using diminutives or other forms of baby talk. He would take time to explain complex concepts to me when I was very young, demonstrating his belief that I could grasp them. As a result, my conversations with my father, until the time of his passing, often sounded more like intellectual exchanges between professional colleagues than father–daughter chats. He, too, appeared to believe that I was born with a gift, and his role was to cultivate this gift in me, even in our common, everyday interactions.

For the first 5 years of my life, I self-identified as intellectually gifted. Messages from my parents, grandparents, and older siblings affirmed and reinforced this self-perception. It was not until the age of 6, as I prepared for the 1st grade at the neighborhood Catholic school, that I began to question this identity through messages I received from school administrators and teachers. My earliest memory is the entrance examination I was required to take for this school. While I do not recall specific questions on the exam, for years I carried with me the failure I felt when leaving the examination room. I remember not sleeping well that night, incessantly reviewing in my mind questions I may have answered incorrectly.

This feeling was confirmed for me when I was eventually admitted to the school.[1] The school placed 1st-graders into groups based on exam results. There were three groups of students—the high, middle, and low groups. I was placed in the middle group, which was very disappointing. Both of my siblings excelled academically, and I had observed how proud this made my parents. In my 6-year-old mind, I had disappointed myself and my entire family. It was at this point I decided I may not be as intelligent as my brother and sister, but I would work harder than both of them and my classmates to make it to the high group.

I did, after a few months. However, my idea of who I was significantly changed in my primary years. I no longer regarded myself as a gifted child. I was a worker. I held onto this idea for the larger part of my academic career, through my middle and high school years, undergrad, and even as I pursued a master's degree at a top historically White institution (HWI). This idea was reinforced (as I saw it) in classroom interactions with my teachers, all of whom were White and regarded me as pleasant, possessing a positive attitude, and showing excellent work habits, as evidenced in their grade report comments

Table 11.1. Grade Report Comments from Teachers in Grades 2–6 (1978–1983)

Year/Grade	Teacher Comments
1978–1979/ Grade 2	I'm sure you must be very proud of Lisa. She has done such excellent work this quarter.
1979–1980/ Grade 3	Lisa is doing very well and has good work habits. She must be encouraged to keep working hard to keep good marks. Lisa is a good student with serious and positive attitude toward her responsibilities to her schoolwork.
1980–1981/ Grade 4	Lisa adds warmth and helpfulness to our class. She is doing fine. Lisa does terrific work. Everything is always carefully and neatly done.
1981–1982/ Grade 5	Lisa exhibits a mature attitude toward her studies. She is a delight to teach.
1982–1983/ Grade 6	Lisa's study habits and conduct are exemplary. Lisa is a responsible student and shows kindness to others. I am pleased with Lisa's interests and efforts in her studies.

(see Table 11.1). My teachers always addressed *what I did* to achieve superior grades, not *who I was* as a gifted person.[2] This distinction mattered to me. Their perceptions of me never quite aligned with those of my parents and elders when describing my academic ability. As much as I needed to hear these words from my teachers, they never came.

Looking back, this cognitive dissonance I experienced bothered me, and I desperately needed to find agreement between the ways in which my family and teachers regarded my intelligence. I therefore abandoned the deeply joyful notion of giftedness given to me by my family, deciding I was who my teachers said I was: a hard worker.

In this book chapter, I explore conflicting messages of giftedness within Black and White cultural contexts. My perspective is informed and supported by the literature on Western/White conceptualizations of intelligence and giftedness, and I juxtapose these ideas with those in communities of color. I then share how after years of self-doubt with regard to my giftedness, I encounter a team of faculty members at a historically Black university (HBCU), who together reconstructed and strengthened my gifted identity. I ground my HBCU experience in an HBCU-based, institution-centric framework that describes the core features that lead to student success.

CULTURALLY CONFLICTING MESSAGES INVOLVING GIFTEDNESS

The notion of academic giftedness in the Western world is both contro-versial and misunderstood. For individuals from communities of color, discussions of giftedness evoke emotional and psychological pain due to subjective, race-laden perspectives that have historically ensued. For instance, educational psychologist Arthur Jensen (1969) assert-ively addressed the issue of race and intelligence in his pivotal essay, *"How much can we boost IQ and scholastic achievement?"* This work was widely cited by eugenicists, Darwinists, and scientists from other pos-itivistic intellectual communities until the 1990s. In this essay, Jensen made several erroneous assumptions about the nature of knowledge, the goal and validity of intelligence testing, and the objectivity of his scholarly inquiry into the relationship between race and intelligence. Nevertheless, he concluded with the following:

> There is an increasing realization among students of the psychology of the disadvantaged that the discrepancy in their average performance cannot be completely or directly attributed to discrimination or inequal-ities in education. It seems not unreasonable, in view of the fact that in-telligence variation has a large genetic component, to hypothesize that genetic factors may play a part in this picture. But such a hypothesis is anathema to many social scientists. The idea that the lower average intelligence and scholastic performance of Negroes could involve, not only environmental, but also genetic, factors has indeed been strongly denounced. But it has been neither contradicted nor discredited by ev-idence. (p. 82)

Jensen's work held significant value among social scientists for de-cades, doing harm in terms of its perspective on the intellectual deficits and cultural disadvantages experienced by Black children. While his work was alarming in its posture as scientific research, his ideas were not unfamiliar in Western ideology, finding roots in the philosophi-cal elucidations of educational thinkers such as Thomas Jefferson and John Dewey. In his seminal work, *Notes on the State of Virginia*, Thom-as Jefferson (1782) devoted considerable effort drawing comparisons between Blacks (then enslaved Africans) and Whites. His awkward descriptions of the biological differences between the two races were unsound, venturing into the preposterous. More disturbing, his ac-count of differences in intelligence grievously kindled racist thought in education, some of which persists today. He wrote:

> Comparing [Blacks] by their faculties of memory, reason, and imagination, it appears to me that in memory they are equal to the whites; in reason, much inferior, as I think one could scarcely be found capable of tracing and comprehending the investigations of Euclid: and that in imagination they are dull, tasteless, and anomalous. (p. 163)

Dewey held similar views of Black people, although scholars have argued a shifting of his perspective toward the end of his life. Fallace (2011) confronts the racism in Dewey's earlier works, noting his positioning of Black people as savages and uncivilized beings. In his opinion, Black people could therefore be regarded as an earlier form of White people, who were far more developed and civilized in all aspects of human development, including intelligence.

There is a strong body of research on giftedness as related to students of color (Ford & Grantham, 2011; Ford et al., 2008; Ford & Webb, 1994; Grantham & Ford, 2003), much of which acknowledges racist ideas in gifted education. Ford and Grantham (2003) explored the presence of negative beliefs about intelligence, race, and culture, as well as "dishonest" research methods among researchers and scientists studying intelligence (p. 218). They argued racist ideas of intelligence, or deficit thinking, could be traced in large part to the underrepresentation of Black and Brown students in gifted programs, describing deficit thinking as occurring "when educators hold negative, stereotypic, and counterproductive views about culturally diverse students and lower their expectations of these students accordingly" (p. 217). They likewise noted several issues in the identification of students of color as gifted, including culturally loaded assessments used to measure intelligence and giftedness; subjective policies and practices, such as teacher referral; and a lack of culturally responsive teachers who are underexposed to gifted instruction, testing, and assessment in teacher education programs.

There is consensus among scholars that no agreed-upon definition of *giftedness* exists. Its presence, however, is acknowledged in almost all cultural and racial groups (Bevan-Brown, 2010; Ford & Grantham, 2003; Ngara & Porath, 2007; Peterson, 1999). These ideas of giftedness are specifically shaped by a cultural group's beliefs, values, language, religion, and attitudinal perspectives. Peterson (1999) further notes that, as with all other social constructions, *giftedness* means different things to different people, "constructed by each person, depending on understandings brought to bear on that person's conceptualization, including cultural factors" (p. 361).

MESSAGES RECEIVED FROM TEACHERS AND ELDERS

As I reflect upon my giftedness, I distinguish my experiences with White teachers[3] from those with my family members. My White teachers held no ill intentions in communicating deficit-based messages to me. They did not intend to purposefully withhold any affirmation of giftedness from me. Still, they did so and I believe this occurred for two reasons. First, I experienced reduced expectations from my teachers based on historically informed perceptions of academic ability and race. I held my teachers in such high regard, and therefore it is uncomfortable for me to retrospectively consider that they enacted a ceiling for my intellectual potential, one much lower than that of my White counterparts. I received messages from them regarding my intellectual inferiority (see Table 11.2), as compared to White students, particularly female students.

My teachers also projected their cultural understanding of giftedness upon me, one which greatly differed from that of my family's in terms of the origin, nature, identification, and purpose of giftedness. They appeared to regard giftedness as a construct that was measured and identified objectively. Since I rarely performed optimally on tests of intelligence or other standardized assessments, I believe my intelligence was greatly underestimated. They also stressed achievement as an individual act, resulting in success for individuals who were motivated and capable. They singled out the few high academic achievers in the class, holding them as models for all other students. All of these students were White.

My parents presented intelligence much differently to me (see Table 11.3). While my parents likewise stressed my individual achievement, they simultaneously emphasized intelligence as a social act, enhanced through social interactions with others. Intelligence was to be nurtured and consistently affirmed in my parents' eyes, which accounts for my mother's constant reminders to me of my "brilliance." Finally, my parents believed that my intelligence was divinely imparted and inspired, and must therefore be used in service to others.

Differences in the ways cultural groups perceive giftedness were captured in Peterson's (1999) enthnographic study on giftedness through various cultural lenses, the findings of which provide insight into my own experiences. In this study, Latinx, Black, Native American, immigrant Asian, and low-income White participants were asked to decide whom they would hypothetically recommend for a gifted

Table 11.2. Negative Messages Received from Teachers Regarding My Intelligence, Across School Levels

School Level	Negative Message
Elementary/ Middle	• Even when testing into advanced reading and math groups, teachers advised me to buddy up with a White female student so I would not fall behind. • Overhearing teachers speak with the high-achieving White female students in familiar, nonformal ways, but still maintaining a sense of distance and formality with me. • Highlighting my work habits to other students ("Students, look how well-behaved Lisa is," "Students, look how Lisa formatted her paper like I asked"); but highlighting White female students' intelligence and insight (i.e., "That's a really smart comment, Miriam. I never thought of it that way")
High	• Not approving me to take Advanced Placement courses which required a high analytical ability, such as AP English Literature, even when I achieved all As and high scores in general English classes. • Calling on me to respond to low-level information/ knowledge questions in class discussions, even when I eagerly demonstrated my desire to attempt to answer higher-order questions. • Choosing me to represent my high school at community events which highlighted my leadership ability, religious practice, temperament, and so on; but not selecting me for events/competitions that required the application of my aptitude/intelligence.

program. There were similarities among individuals from the communities of colors, which included a family and social orientation toward giftedness, various artistic abilities, and "nonbook" knowledge (p. 371). Interestingly, Native American individuals refused to ascribe the label of giftedness, expressing it as wrongful to place someone in a higher position than others.

White teachers, on the other hand, tended to associate giftedness with a well-developed work ethic, motivation, and individual achievement. When considering the giftedness of students of color, there was a tendency among White teachers to qualify students' academic gifts. For example, one White teacher discussed a Native American student's artistic ability, but qualified by stating the student, was "not very good in math" (Peterson, 1999, p. 373).

Table 11.3. Differences in Cultural Beliefs Between My Parents and Teachers Regarding Giftedness

Element of Giftedness	Parental Beliefs	Teacher Beliefs
The Origin of Giftedness (Ngara, 2013; Ngara & Porath, 2007; Peterson, 1999)	Bestowed by God	Has genetic, racial, and cultural implications
The Nature of Giftedness (Ford & Grantham, 2003)	Provided by God, but must be nurtured and cultivated under the guidance of adults	Fixed and possessed by only a few
How Giftedness is Identified (Ngara & Porath, 2007)	Primarily through parental observation and social interactions with others	Through objective measurements
The Purpose of Giftedness (Ngara, 2013; Ngara & Porath, 2007; Peterson, 1999)	To uplift and serve others	To achieve goals as individuals

Expanding Western ideas of intelligence gained traction in both education research and practice with the introduction of Gardner's (1983) theory of multiple intelligences. However, giftedness from a global perspective—involving the identification of giftedness in non-quantifiable terms, examinations of giftedness from ontological and spiritual perspectives, and diverse manifestations of giftedness—existed well before Gardner's work. A review of a few cultural studies related to giftedness (Chandler, 2010; Ngara, 2013; Ngara & Porath, 2007) reveals diverse understandings, such as the Maori culture, which contends a holistic orientation toward interpersonal relations when identifying giftedness; the Keresa Pueblo Indian culture, which believes that gifted individuals best reflect the culture's values, beliefs, and behaviors; and the Aboriginal people of Canada, who believe that everyone has a gift and "the real purpose of life is therefore to find one's gift and then use it wisely for the benefit of others around you" (Ngara & Porath, 2007, p. 194).

Ngara and Porath (2007) found "diverse gifted students' cultural views may impact negatively on both their identification and achievement in Western-oriented gifted education programs" (p. 194). They conducted a pioneer study that explored a sub-Saharan African worldview of giftedness as expressed in the Ndebele culture of Zimbabwe. Findings from a questionnaire given to 30 Ndebele teachers revealed giftedness as an "unusually outstanding ability blessed in an individual from birth, which manifests itself in amazing competencies and expertise, including creativity" (p. 199). Giftedness was also believed to be collectively owned, and wisdom was greatly valued as a companion to high intelligence among gifted individuals. Finally, giftedness was seen as a spiritual blessing that can be taken away if underused or exploited. These findings supported earlier research findings conducted among the Shona people of Zimbabwe, where giftedness was viewed as a divine provision, given to each individual in the culture in a unique way; an expression of extra-cognitive abilities; and possessing a social orientation (Ngara, 2013).

Perhaps Chandler (2010) best captured the cultural conflict I experienced when speaking about his own experience as an Aboriginal man confronting dominant cultural ideas of giftedness in Australia. We shared similar identities as school-age children (i.e., hard workers versus gifted students), although we lived on two different continents. This similarity, however, was grounded in the need to make sense of our identities within Western contexts, as children with deeply embedded cultural values and beliefs. We were also similarly reinforced by our teachers' perceptions of us, documented in grade reports we both reviewed years later. Chandler wrote:

> My first non-Aboriginal mentor was somebody called Miraca Gross, the founder of The Gifted Education Research, Resource, and Information Centre. When I first met Miraca at the School of Education at the University of NSW as a PhD student, she indicated to me that she felt I was a child prodigy, that I was a gifted child who was never identified at school. I indicated to her that I was more like a problem child and, as evidence, showed her all my school reports. Two very different perspectives. How could someone who was the first person in their family to finish primary school end up being one of Australia's ten top researchers? Miraca said that it was because I was gifted. I said I worked hard. And that rigorous and academic debate went back many years. (pp. 1–2)

Despite these conflicting messages, I achieved very high grades through the 12th grade, and average grades in my undergraduate and master's-level work. Internally, however, I faced feelings of inferiority, particularly as compared to the White students who learned alongside of me. It was not until the age of 29 when I encountered a group of teachers who genuinely saw me as gifted. It was the beginning of a liberating reality for me, one which has shaped both my professional trajectory and life's path.

THE BEGINNING OF AN AFFIRMING JOURNEY
AT HOWARD UNIVERSITY

After 5 years of teaching at a high school in Maryland, I decided to attend Howard University in order to earn my administrative certification. I did not have a particularly strong desire to be a school administrator. I was more intrigued by the idea of attending Howard University. The Educational Administration and Policy program had a 30-credit hour program that would allow me to earn my certification in 2 years. After attending the University of Virginia (UVA), an HWI with a persistently racialized climate often filled with overt hostility, I craved a more inclusive, welcoming educational experience. As a native Washingtonian, I was aware that Howard University had the potential to fill this need as it had for many of my family members, friends, and colleagues. My experience in this program was relatively uneventful until my final semester, when I enrolled in R. C. Saravanabhavan's (Dr. RC) Organizational Change course. This course was a doctoral-level course, but as a certification student, my academic advisor permitted me to take it since I performed well in previous courses.

Enrolling in a doctoral course was quite intimidating. Having performed successfully in my lower-level courses, I rediscovered the academic confidence I lost while at UVA. However, latent feelings of intellectual inferiority were always present, and I doubted my ability to "keep up" with the doctoral students in the course. I found Dr. RC to be a kind and gentle man, a deeply knowledgeable researcher, and an exceptional teacher. A man of Indian descent, Dr. RC brought a compelling global perspective to our class. The way in which he interacted with me as his student demonstrated that he held a great deal of respect for me. When I participated in class discussions, he appeared to truly value my thoughts and perspective. He also appeared to be very proud of my academic prowess in my initial interactions with him, and for the first time in my academic career, I felt *seen* by a teacher, and I began my journey back to the 6-year-old gifted student filled with self-confidence and a desire to use my gift to help others, just as my mother directed.

I never would have earned the doctorate without the support of Dr. RC. He was so impressed with my performance in his class that he offered me a full fellowship to enroll in the doctoral program. He included a graduate assistantship, which allowed me to take a sabbatical from teaching and enroll full-time in the program. He then served as my dissertation chairperson, challenging me to explore complex research methodologies and inspiring in me a love of research that has yet to dissipate. When I first met him, I regarded his impactful presence in my life as anomalous. I would soon learn, however, that he was one arm of a much larger body of departmental faculty who were connected by a common mission and institutional culture and would collectively affirm my giftedness in profound ways.

HBCUS: BACKGROUND AND CONTEXT

Howard University, affectionately known as the Mecca, is considered to be among the top HBCUs in the United States. HBCUs are institutions originally founded to educate Black Americans for industrial enterprises, teaching, and the ministry. Their creation lies in direct opposition to racism and other forms of anti-Blackness and oppression (Grillo et al., 2017; Williams et al., 2019). They were created and promoted by the White establishment to appease Black folks, prevent them from integrating into HWIs, and primarily train them for occupations that would likely maintain their inferior status (Abelman & Delessandro, 2009). Founded after the Civil War primarily by the federal government's Freedman's Bureau, abolitionist missionaries, religious-based organizations, and philanthropists, the common mission of HBCUs also included promoting justice for marginalized groups through professional and community organizing and service (Darrell et al., 2016; Grillo et al., 2017). HBCUs have a shared history of both struggle and victory, a mission of racial advancement, structures and an institutional culture that provide social capital to marginalized and excluded populations, and an educational experience not able to be found at HWIs (Arroyo & Gasman, 2014).

According to the United Negro College Fund, HBCUs awarded 26% of all bachelor's degrees and 32% of STEM degrees earned by Black students in 2016 (Saunders & Nagle, 2018). In states with relatively high numbers of HBCUs, their impact is undeniably large. In North Carolina, for example, HBCUs are 16% of all 4-year institutions, but enroll 45% of all Black undergraduates and award 43% of all Black bachelor's degrees in the state (Saunders & Nagle, 2018). In terms of their larger impact in American society, HBCUs have demonstrably contributed to the growth of the Black middle class in the United States, as 80% of Black officers in the United States military,

80% of Black federal judges, 65% of Black physicians, 60% of Black attorneys, 50% of Black teachers and engineers, and so far, 100% of Black U.S. vice presidents are HBCU graduates (Abelman & Delessandro, 2009).

The significant influence and impact of HBCUs on the larger society is well noted. They have likewise received criticism regarding issues with quality, organizational dysfunction, limited resource availability, and accreditation challenges (Abelman & Delessandro, 2009). Additional criticisms involve their conservative cultures, which force student adherence to gender and sexuality expectations, hair and clothing expectations, and the silencing of opinions and beliefs that conflict with typical mainstream views (Goings, 2016; Njoku et al., 2017). Williams et al. (2019) note that critical narratives of HBCUs lack context and are often rooted in deficit thinking and anti-Black racism.

Despite such criticism, HBCUs have persisted as highly successful and relatively stable institutions, a remarkable feat in light of the fact that they were not designed to succeed (Abelman & Delessandro, 2009). The literature illuminates quite powerfully the unique benefits HBCUs provide to students who are traditionally underserved and marginalized. These benefits are related to the ways in which these institutions provide supportive environments, help students to form academic and racial identities, and facilitate healthy value systems, among others (Arroyo & Gasman, 2014; Darrell et al., 2016; Goings, 2016; Palmer & Gasman, 2008).

AFFIRMATIONS ABOUND AT THE MECCA

One evening after class during my second semester in the doctoral program, I walked across campus to my car with my professor, Jerome Jones, as he headed to the train station. During the course of our conversation, he asked me how my other courses were progressing. I shared with him that I was taking my first course alongside MBA students in the Howard School of Business. I chose to focus on organizational management as my cognate (major) area of study and therefore took 12 credit hours in the MBA program. I explained I was excelling in my online course—a learning format that was new to me—more so than my classmates due to the excessive time I devoted to the course. Dr. Jones smiled. He paused for a moment and then calmly stated, "This may be so, but you are excelling because you are academically gifted." We then proceeded to have a small debate about my natural ability versus my academic work ethic. Dr. Jones shared that I was more advanced than other students. He called me "naturally gifted." I argued that I spent an atypical amount of time on my studies. I listened to him as he continued to speak about my ability and performance in his class. Admittedly, I was a bit overwhelmed by his words because hearing such thoughts from a teacher was a foreign experience for me.

This short, informal conversation was epiphanic for me. It was instrumental in the reclamation of my academic identity as a gifted student. Dr. Jones's words struck me so sharply because I held deep respect for him. I considered him a brilliant man. He held a doctorate in education, a law degree, and a master's degree in urban planning. He was one of the first Black Americans to serve as superintendent in a large, urban school district. He was widely respected in the educational field nationally. I was humbled by his intellect, and more so by his confidence in his intellect. As a student in his class, he made me feel proud to be a Black academic. When I achieved high grades in his course, I knew the grade was well earned. Essentially, if Dr. Jones said I was gifted, I was indeed gifted.

As I progressed in the program, I blossomed intellectually. I spent hours in the "stacks," the dungeon-like rooms in the university library, reading educational journals and seminal texts in my field and beyond. I read Cheikh Anta Diop, Molefi Asante, Asa Hilliard, Lisa Delpit, Paolo Freire, Carter G. Woodson, Frances Cress Welsing, and Na'im Akbar. I also developed an interest in reading key works by Western philosophers and thinkers such as John Locke, Adam Smith, and John Dewey, in an attempt to better understand the philosophical foundations upon which public education was built. I decided to explore Locke's social contract theory and asked one of my professors, Peter Sola, to help me further develop a paper I wrote which interrogated Locke's ideas. Dr. Sola agreed and pushed me to present the paper at the annual Values and Leadership Conference sponsored by the Consortium for the Study of Leadership and Ethics in Education in Pittsburgh. I was intimidated by this proposition, knowing presenters and attendees at this conference were mostly White and male. Dr. Sola sensed my reticence and offered to drive me to the conference and copresent. As a White male scholar who held a fierce commitment to social justice, not only did Dr. Sola feel comfortable in spaces occupied by White men, but also enjoyed challenging their ideas. I loved to watch him in action during these debates.

We traveled to the conference together. The morning of the presentation, he calmly said to me, "I think you can handle this on your own." So nervously, I presented "our" paper on my own while he sat in front of me, nodding in approval. I can still see his eyes as I presented, communicating to me, "You've got this." Years later as an executive in education, when I found myself often in all-White male spaces, I would remember this experience with Dr. Sola and draw confidence from it.

While the experiences with my male professors shaped my gifted identity, my interactions with the only Black female professor in the program solidified it. A former school superintendent in Richmond, Virginia, and Boston, Massachusetts, as well as a former associate professor at Harvard University, Lois Harrison-Jones was an extraordinarily accomplished scholar and educational leader. As my professor, she was tough but fair. She required a great deal from me academically and always provided honest, well-intentioned feedback. In class, she called on me to provide my perspective on various leadership topics, showing genuine interest in my responses. She also grew my leadership, challenging me to take on leadership roles as a graduate student in the School of Education. I felt wholly affirmed by her. Most importantly, by watching her, I learned how to effectively assert myself as both scholar and leader.

While Dr. Harrison-Jones prepared me for the sexism and racism I would experience in this world as a Black woman, she likewise encouraged me to approach life with grace and free of resentment. I watched as she navigated all-male spaces, not allowing herself to be silenced. She knew she was often among the most knowledgeable and wisest in professional settings, and she spoke with authority in disarming, hospitable ways. Her style of leadership was visionary, efficacious and service-oriented. Later, I would model my own leadership after hers.

HBCUS' INVESTMENTS IN STUDENTS

I do not consider my experiences with faculty members as a sum of individual occurrences that inadvertently resulted in a transformative experience for me. I see a coalescence of individuals within a larger institutional cultural context, acting as a purposeful collective body. This institution-centric orientation was explored by Arroyo and Gasman (2014) in the first of its kind model on Black student success within HBCUs. Looking at success at the institutional level, as opposed to the student level, the model focused primarily on the experiences of undergraduate students, but maintained applicability for me as a doctoral student. Based on a synthesis of the literature regarding the contributions of HBCUs, the model described specific HBCU features from an Afrocentric perspective. Researchers rejected the notion of homogeneity among HBCUs, but did offer common institutional features of HBCUs that result in Black students experiencing outcomes of success. The institutional features most aligned to my interactions at Howard include a supportive environment and identity formation (i.e., racial-ethnic, intellectual, and leadership).

The support provided to me by my professors was invaluable. I credit this support with my ability to graduate with a 4.0 grade point average, reshape and fortify my identities as a Black woman and scholar, and develop the leadership that would foundationally allow me to obtain and experience success in executive leadership positions in education. Similarly, Arroyo and Gasman's (2014) institutional model demonstrated that HBCUs provide prolonged opportunities for students to form meaningful relationships with one another, professors, and administrators, which they are able to leverage toward their academic success. Other studies reflect similar findings. For example, in a study of 11 Black undergraduate men at a public, doctoral research-intensive HBCU in the mid-Atlantic part of the United States, Palmer and Gasman (2008) revealed, among other findings, that both professors and administrators were accessible to students, empathetic, supportive of their academic success, and focused on students' personal well-being. Darrell et al. (2016) described the sense of family in HBCU settings, whereby students were seen as kin by adults. Pointing out a difference in experience between HBCUs and HWIs for social work students, researcher Linda Darrell reflected upon her orientation to an HWI as "factual, nonfamilial, and singular" (p. 46). Students in HWIs often experience various forms of racial tension, isolation, silencing, invisibility in the classroom, and academic invalidation. On the other hand, as an institutional practice, "the nurturing context of HBCUs facilitates safe spaces for innovation, excellence, conversation, affirming, learning, teaching, and the development of a genuine relationship and connection between and among faculty and students" (p. 44). Darrell et al. referred to this as a "transformative experience" for students.

My Howard experience debunked any deficit-based notion I may have held regarding the mutual exclusivity between Blackness and intelligence. At Howard, I interacted with the most brilliant minds I had ever met. Many of these individuals were also unapologetically Black, expressly committed to Black upliftment, and believing in the ingenuity and excellence of Black people. I therefore underwent a process where both my intelligence and racial identifies were thoroughly affirmed and integrated, helping me to reach a higher sense of self. The idea of intellectual and racial identity formation among Black students across the educational pipeline is likewise addressed in the literature (Arroyo & Gasman, 2014; Darrell et al., 2016; Goings, 2016). The formation of identity (i.e., racial-ethnic, intellectual, and leadership) within HBCUs is uniquely achieved through the integration of traditional methodologies with culturally relevant pedagogical practices; the active presence of Black professors; a shared commitment among HBCU presidents and other leaders to nurture and support student leadership development; and external role models interacting with the institution.

Goings (2016) used Whiting's scholar identity model to explore the academic and social experiences of two undergraduate Black men at HBCUs varying in size and location. These two young men developed a scholar identity composed of self-efficacy, academic self-confidence, and a racial consciousness. Participants expressed a high degree of support in the form of "intellectual nurturing" (p. 65) from their professors, resulting in their academic success. Darrell et al. (2016) explored racial identity in terms of students' understanding the historical struggle to achieve racial and economic equality and equity, which empowered them to join in the fight toward these ideals. They noted, "The affirmation of racial identity is a key factor in the success of African American students and other students of color. The nurturing experience of an HBCU results from a foundation of service in which a safe space is created through constantly exposing students to microaffirmations emanating from relationships with faculty, peers, and alumni" (p. 45).

DISCUSSION, IMPLICATIONS, AND RECOMMENDATIONS FOR PRACTICE

According to Jones et al. (2016), autoethnographies use personal experience to examine, interrogate, and critique cultural experience. As a research method, autoenthnographies share a few common characteristics, which include "(1) purposefully commenting on/ critiquing of culture and cultural practices, (2) making contributions to existing research, (3) embracing vulnerability with purpose, and (4) creating a reciprocal relationship with audiences in order to compel a response" (p. 22).

In this autoethnography I situate my personal experience with cultural messaging around giftedness within a social scientific inquiry. Most giftedness research related to students of color acts as an advocatory tool for students by presenting the perspectives of professionals and scholars. This study, however, retrospectively examines the issue through a student lens. I explore (and emotionally expose) the ways in which I incongruently experience giftedness within two cultural contexts and the resulting mixed messages, which led to an identity conflict. I offer a new perspective on how conflicting cultural messages manifest throughout the academic career of a nonidentified gifted student. Further research on the ways in which students experience their own giftedness and intelligence would add depth to this line of inquiry, potentially engendering a deeper understanding of the impact of policies and practices in gifted education (and beyond) at the student-level.

This chapter also provides actionable implications regarding the preparation of preservice teachers in higher education, as well as the development of teacher capacity in school districts, as we seek to respond to increasingly diverse student populations in culturally responsive ways. First and foremost, professionals in higher education and school districts responsible for preparing and developing teachers should interrogate the underlying assumptions embedded in their program content and pedagogy. For example, teachers may be taught that there are students of color in their classrooms with unidentified learning deficits, and who therefore may require teaching approaches beyond those in a typical general education classroom environment. Are teachers taught the same regarding gifted students? Learning needs should be viewed on a continuum that includes giftedness as well as "dis-ability." Likewise, are teachers encouraged to explore culturally informed notions of giftedness to construct a more holistic understanding? It is important to constantly unearth and confront assumptions rooted in intellectual and cultural inferiority. The preparation and development of teachers across grade levels, disciplines, and areas of specialization should therefore include the following opportunities for teachers:

1. Constructive self-reflection on assumptions and biases they may hold regarding intelligence and ability, as related to race and culture
2. Exploration of these concepts through several racial and cultural lenses
3. Listening to the voices of students of color related to giftedness, whether they are identified or unidentified as gifted
4. Strategies to identify giftedness beyond objective measures
5. Innovative pedagogical and curricular approaches for gifted students of color

In addition to my contribution to giftedness research, this study supports a growing body of asset-oriented literature that speaks to the significance and importance of HBCUs. Amid reports of declining enrollments, funding issues, incompetent leadership, and other factors that potentially threaten the viability and sustainability of these institutions (Williams et al., 2019), this research adds much-needed balance to this discourse. One recommendation for future research related to this topic is to explore the experiences of identified gifted students (across undergraduate and graduate programs) in HBCUs using case study methods in order to ascertain, thorough prolonged engagement, if and how their academic and social–emotional needs were met. Understanding how to meet the unique needs of specific groups of students is critical as HBCUs commit to constant academic program improvement.

NOTES

1. I did not attend kindergarten regularly, as my brother and sister did (kindergarten was not required by the state in which I lived at the time). Therefore, I likely missed important concepts covered on the entrance exam. As an intensely introverted child, I found kindergarten quite anxiety-producing; I preferred to remain in the care of my grandmother, whom I adored. My parents, therefore, did not force my regular attendance. On my kindergarten progress report, my teacher noted, "Lisa is making good progress, regardless of her long absences. I am pleased that she grasps new concepts quickly. She tends to be quiet and shy in our room . . . she rarely participates in group discussions unless called upon."

2. Gifted was not a formal designation used at my Catholic school. It was informally used among teachers to denote students with high academic ability, a high aptitude, or superior intelligence. Other terms, such as accelerated,

were also used; however, I do not recall a teacher using any such terms to describe me

3. Throughout my life, I estimate I have had 55 teachers until I reached my post-master's work. Three of these teachers were Black. All others were White (95%). From grades kindergarten through 12, I had one Black teacher. During my undergraduate and master's level studies at the University of Virginia, I had a Black male Spanish professor, and I took a seminar course with the late civil rights leader Julian Bond.

REFERENCES

Abelman, R., & Delessandro, A. (2009). The institutional vision of historically Black colleges and universities. *Journal of Black Studies, 40*(2), 105–134.

Arroyo, A. T., & Gasman, M. (2014). An HBCU-based educational approach for Black college student success: Toward a framework with implications for all institutions. *American Journal of Education, 121*(1), 57–85. https://doi.org/10.1086/678112

Bevan-Brown, J. (2010, July 29–August 1). *Indigenous conceptions of giftedness* [Paper presentation]. 11th Asia Pacific Conference on Giftedness, Sydney, NSW, Australia.

Chandler, P. (2010, July 29–August 1). *Prodigy or problem child? Challenges with identifying Aboriginal giftedness* [Paper presentation]. 11th Asia Pacific Conference on Giftedness, Sydney, NSW, Australia.

Darrell, L., Littlefield, M., & Washington, E. M. (2016). Safe spaces, nurturing places. *Journal of Social Work Education, 52*(1), 43–49. https://doi.org/10.1080/10437797.2016.1119016

Fallace, T. D. (2011). *Dewey and the dilemma of race: An intellectual history, 1895–1922.* Teachers College Press.

Ford, D. Y., & Grantham, T. C. (2003). Providing access for culturally diverse gifted students: From deficit to dynamic thinking. *Theory Into Practice, 42*(3), 217–225.

Ford, D. Y., & Grantham, T. C. (Eds.). (2011). *Using the NAGC programming standards to create program and services for culturally and linguistically different gifted students.* Prufrock Press.

Ford, D. Y., Grantham, T. C., & Whiting, G. W. (2008). Culturally and linguistically diverse students in gifted education: Recruitment and retention issues. *Exceptional Children, 74*(3), 289–306. https://doi.org/10.1177%2F001440290807400302

Ford, D. Y., & Webb, K. S. (1994). Desegregation of gifted educational programs: The impact of Brown on underachieving children of color. *The Journal of Negro Education, 63*(3), 358–375.

Gardner, H. (1983). *Frames of mind: Theory of multiple intelligences.* Basic Books.

Goings, R. B. (2016). Investigating the experiences of two high-achieving Black male HBCU graduates: An exploratory study. *The Negro Educational Review, 67*(1–4), 54–75.

Grantham, T. C., & Ford, D. Y. (2003). Beyond self-concept and self-esteem for African American students: Improving racial identity improves achievement. *The High School Journal, 87*(1), 18–29. https://doi.org/10.1353/hsj.2003.0016

Grillo, L. M., Ellis, A. L., & Durham, J. D. (2017). Continuing HBCU's historical commitment to personnel preparation: Preparing transition professionals to serve students of color with disabilities. *Perspectives on Urban Education, 14*(1), 1–5. Retrieved from https://files.eric.ed.gov/fulltext/EJ1160506.pdf

Jefferson, T. (1782). *Notes on the state of Virginia.* In T. F. P. Project (Ed.).

Jensen, A. R. (1969). How much can we boost IQ and scholastic achievement? *Harvard Educational Review, 39*(1), 1–123.

Jones, S. H., Adams, T. E., & Ellis, C. (Eds.). (2016). *Handbook of autoethnography.* Routledge.

Ngara, C. (2013). The talent development model: An African perspective of Shona culture. *Talent Development and Excellence, 5*(2), 23–30.

Ngara, C., & Porath, M. (2007). Ndebele culture of Zimbabwe's views of giftedness. *High Ability Studies, 18*(2), 191–208. https://doi.org/10.1080/13598130701709566

Njoku, N., Butler, M., & Beatty, C. C. (2017). Reimagining the historically Black college and university (HBCU) environment: Exposing race secrets and the binding chains of respectability and othermothering. *International Journal of Qualitative Studies in Education, 30*(8), 783–799.

Palmer, R. T., & Gasman, M. (2008). "It takes a village to raise a child": The role of social capital in promoting academic success for African American men at a Black college. *Journal of College Student Development, 49*(1), 52–70.

Peterson, J. S. (1999). Gifted—through whose cultural lens? An application of the postpositivistic mode of inquiry. *Journal for the Education of the Gifted, 22*(4), 354–383.

Saunders, K. M., & Nagle, B. T. (2018). *HBCUs punching above their weight: A state-level analysis of historically Black college and university enrollment and graduation.* UNCF Frederick D. Patterson Research Institute. https://cdn.uncf.org/wp-content/uploads/PATW_Report_FINAL0919.pdf?_ga=2.225038546.991204843.1605643937-2107748169.1605643937

Williams, K. L., Burt, B. A., Clay, K. L., & Bridges, B. K. (2019). Stories untold: Counter-narratives to anti-blackness and deficit-oriented discourse concerning HBCUs. *American Educational Research Journal, 56*(2), 556–599.

CHAPTER 12

¿No me ves?

Seen by Two Teachers in a Sea of Blind Educators

Aimeé I. Cepeda

While preparing to write this chapter, I reflected on the overwhelming shock I experienced as an Afro-Latina student when I transitioned to the American public school system in the early 1980s from a culturally responsive environment to one that is infected with racism, classism, and other biases against students from non-White cultures. My 1st- through 7th-grade education was facilitated by teachers who shared my pride of being *Boricua* (Puerto Rican). In addition, they lived in my community and I would often run into them at the grocery store, at the beach, and around the community. They had great relationships with my immediate family. They visited my home before I knew what home visits were, and they shared their *cariño* (affection) broadly with me. One such teacher was Misis (Ms.) Tapia, my 1st-grade teacher. In that regard, studies suggest that teachers who have developed successful partnerships with families view students' academic, career, and personal/social development as a shared responsibility among all stakeholders—for example, caregivers, family members, administrators, teachers, school support personnel, and the community (ASCA, 2003; Ellis, 2019, p. xi). However, as happy as my education was *en mi isla* (on my island), my transition to the American education system was equally traumatic.

Soon after arriving in the United States, I began to feel like a burden to teachers, who were frustrated with the fact that I could not speak English. Most of my teachers could not see past my inability to understand what they were saying because they were speaking a language completely foreign to me. Various studies have researched teacher quality and the preparation of public school teachers. A significant and relevant finding of L. Lewis et al. (1999) was that while 54% of teachers taught English language learners (ELLs) or culturally diverse students, only 20% felt adequately prepared to teach them. I vividly remember a very painful experience during my first day of school in 8th grade. My limited English education in Puerto Rico prepared me to answer questions like "What is your name?" "How old are you?" and "Where do you live?" But I was completely unprepared to answer my teacher's request to spell my name. I understood the word *name* and continued to answer *Aimeé Cepeda*. Every time the teacher asked me to spell my name, she became more and more flustered with my response. Completely undone by my inability to answer her question, my teacher asked me to sit down, which I understood. I felt unwanted and unwelcome, and yearned to return to *mi isla y mi cultura* (my island and my culture). It wasn't until I met Ms. Gershowitz, my first English for speakers of other languages (ESOL) teacher that I felt a sense of compassion and acceptance. She explained to me what *spell* meant and taught me how to spell my name.

Not much has changed in the experiences that ELLs face when they enter American classrooms. Research suggests that teachers may be concerned about (1) chronic lack of time to address ELLs' unique classroom needs (Youngs, 1999), (b) perceived intensification of teacher workloads when ELLs are enrolled in mainstream classes (Gitlin et al., 2003), and (c) feelings of professional inadequacy to work with ELLs (Verplaetse, 1998). In terms of the impact of inclusion on the classroom learning environment, teachers are concerned about the possibility that ELLs will slow the class progression through the curriculum (Youngs, 1999) or result in inequities in educational opportunities for all students (Platt et al., 2003; Reeves, 2004; Schmidt, 2000). Finally, some evidence of the attitudes and perceptions of ELLs held by subject area teachers is present in research, including a reluctance to work with low-proficiency ELLs (Platt et al., 2003), misconceptions about the processes of second-language acquisition (Olsen, 1997; Reeves, 2004; Walqui, 2000), and assumptions (positive and negative) about the race and ethnicity of ELLs (Harklau, 2000; Valdes, 2001; Vollmer, 2000).

The institutional racism ELLs experience daily destroys aspirations they may have to achieve the American dream (Bonilla-Silva, 2017). "Personal experiences with discrimination in combination with institutional mistrust can contribute to feelings of alienation and academic disengagement" (Benner & Graham, 2011, p. 509) for students of color. Feeling dehumanized and disconnected, many Latinx students choose to drop out of school. I am grateful to have had extraordinary teachers like Ms. Tapia and Ms. Gershowitz who saw my worth and invested in me and gave me the tools needed to persevere through the struggles.

In two different periods of my life, these teachers engaged in similar practices. Each bonded with me and learned from me information they would use to help me succeed in school and in life. Ladson-Billings (1995) defines their practices as "good teaching": building authentic bonds with students, in school and in the community, by creating environments where students succeed and teaching them to embrace learning by providing them with individual attention and encouragement that awakens self-consciousness.

My story as a scholar originates with the lessons learned from Ms. Tapia, my 1st-grade teacher in Puerto Rico. Lessons of discipline and grit, behaviors applicable to everything in my life. The story advances with the lessons learned from Ms. Gershowitz, my first ESOL teacher when I moved to the United States from Puerto Rico. Lessons of trust, compassion, and self-acceptance. These two teachers saw in me what I did not see in myself until many years later, the ability to debunk the prejudiced limitations placed on me by others. Their ability to "see" me taught me to see myself, elevate my worth, and pay it forward by "seeing" the students and teachers I lead and educate every day. It is my hope that my story will empower teachers to "see" their students beyond their color, culture, or academic performance, and to spark a passion in them that will last a lifetime.

A CULTURALLY RESPONSIVE CLASSROOM EXPERIENCE: LESSONS LEARNED FROM MS. TAPIA

As I reflect on all that I have accomplished as a scholar, I wish I could go home to thank Ms. Tapia, my 1st-grade teacher in La Escuela Elemental Amapolas, Guaynabo, Puerto Rico. The school and Ms. Tapia are long gone, but the lessons I learned in her class have remained with me always. Ms. Tapia was a seasoned teacher, older than most teachers in the school. She reminded me very much of my grandmother, nurturing and stern. Every day began with Ms. Tapia greeting me at her door with a warm smile and a hug. She treated every student with love and compassion, even when we disobeyed the rules of her classroom. Whenever this happened, as it happened to me once or twice, Ms. Tapia had me write on the board, *No voy a hablar* (I'm not going to talk) during recess, for what seemed to me like an eternity. As a 6-year-old child, this seemed like cruel punishment, and I cried.

Ms. Tapia consoled me and explained gently that if she let me talk during class, I would continue to do it and I would miss the lesson. However, she offered me a solution, to wait until lunch or recess to talk with my classmates. That way I would pay attention in class and not miss recess. The next day, Ms. Tapia reminded me of her expectation as I entered her classroom early that morning. Throughout the day, she glanced at me and winked with a smile to let me know I was doing a good job remaining focused. At dismissal, Ms. Tapia hugged me and told me how proud she was of me for not talking during class and for staying focused. She then told me that because I was such a good student that day, she knew I could do it every day and that she wanted me to try very hard to be a model student. She often praised my behavior to let other students know how she wanted them to behave in class. Researchers contend that teacher's praise is contingent on and explicitly linked to class and student behaviors that the teacher wishes to increase (T. J. Lewis et al., 2004; McKerchar & Thompson, 2004; Moore Partin et al., 2009). Every time she did this, I felt proud of my accomplishment and tried even harder, not just to remain quiet, but to do the best work and to earn the best grades in the class.

I did not understand it then, but Ms. Tapia was teaching me discipline and grit through social interaction. She was teaching me to adhere to the code of behavior in her classroom, first with a negative consequence to get my attention, and then with restorative justice to sustain my observance of the classroom rules. "Restorative justice is a powerful approach to discipline that focuses on repairing harm through inclusive processes that engage all stakeholders. Implemented well, RJ shifts the focus of discipline from punishment to learning and from the individual to the community" (Ferlazzo, 2006, p. 2). In giving me the opportunity to correct my own behavior, she made me feel emotionally safe to make mistakes and try again while modeling for me and teaching me the values she required me to practice in her classroom community. The positive social interaction between Ms. Tapia and me led to my positive social and emotional development during my very first experience with formal education and sparked a passion for learning that has remained with me throughout my entire academic career.

Ms. Tapia's behavior management strategies fostered a warm and welcoming climate where I could learn and thrive. She did so by giving me a choice to correct my behavior and by using positive

consequences that granted opportunity for restitution. Effective behavioral management is generally based on the principle of establishing a positive classroom environment encompassing effective
teacher–student relationships (Wubbels et al., 1999). Ms. Tapia saw in
me a desire to please her and capitalized on my desire by empowering
me to engage in long-term self-regulation strategies. While that was
not my experience with every teacher during my formative years, it
was a lesson that I have carried with me all of my life. Unfortunately, most students do not experience learning environments of social
excellence. It is well documented that Latinx and African American
students are more likely to receive a discipline referral than White students for the same behavior (Skiba et al., 2011). In taking a transac-
tional approach to discipline, teachers fail to address the root cause of
the behavior or to repair the harm caused by exclusionary discipline.
Delpit (1995) describes how cultural divergence between White educators and students of color impacts the experiences for these students
(p. 73). Students of color are less likely to receive positive feedback
and are assumed to lack the skill or motivation to do well in school,
which often becomes a self-fulfilling prophecy for students when educators deposit *"absolute ignorance"* into the minds of their students
(Freire, 1968/1972).

FROM TURMOIL TO CONFIDENCE:
LESSONS LEARNED FROM MS. GERSHOWITZ

Latinx are the fastest-growing group of students enrolled in public schools, yet over 80% of teachers are White (National Center for
Education Statistics, 2019). I was one of those students transitioning
to a U.S. middle school in the early 1980s who only had two non-
White teachers to interact with during the day. One of those was Ms.
Gershowitz, a young Jewish teacher who spoke fluent Spanish. Ms.
Gershowitz was well aware of how scary the drastic change to a new
country, new school, new culture, and new language would be for her
students. She was very invested in teaching her ESOL students how to
cope with the changes by creating a classroom community that fostered
trust, compassion, and self-acceptance. Ms. Gershowitz celebrated our
similarities instead of our differences. I remember her introducing me
to the other students in my ESOL class who were Dominican, Salva-
dorian, and Columbian. With such an array of skin tones, features, and
cultures, Ms. Gershowitz focused on the fact that we all spoke Spanish

and that we were all engaging on a journey that would require us to support and protect each other. I remember the first few assignments in her class were about my classmates and me introducing each other to our place of birth, our families, and our culture.

We shared stories and pictures of our childhood back home. We talked about our families and the food we loved. I shared how I missed going to the beach after school to do my homework and how much I missed *mis abuelas* (my grandmothers). That opened up the conversation between my classmates and me when we all learned how close we were to our *abuelas* and how we all yearned to be back home with them. In our vulnerability of being foreigners in a new land, we began to bond, and the six of us—Rosemary, Edwin, Pedro, Flerida, Manuel, and I—were inseparable. This bond was extremely important to me, because as a dark *Boricua* some students in the school would question my ethnicity. Once in Social Studies class, a boy asked Flerida how I could be Puerto Rican if I did not have white skin and straight hair. Flerida translated the statement for me, and seeing how the comment made me feel inadequate, she responded before I could gather my thoughts. "*Estupidos!* We all come in different colors and sizes just like you!" My friends accepted me unconditionally and defended me whenever someone would say something about me that I could not understand or respond to.

Ms. Gershowitz also taught us to support each other. Whoever was best in a particular subject had the responsibility to teach everyone else, in Spanish and English: in Spanish so we would understand the concepts deeply, and in English so we could learn the terms and the vocabulary. Over the school year, as we became more fluent in English, Ms. Gershowitz challenged us to participate in other classes, something I did not want to do because of my heavy Spanish accent. She explained that the more I spoke in English, the faster others would learn to understand my accent. Her expectation was not for me to lose my accent, but for others to learn to accept it. That was a game changer for me. I began to speak Spanglish in her class, saying the words I knew in English mixed with the ones I did not know in Spanish. She would repeat what I was trying to say in full English and then would ask me to repeat it. Ms. Gershowitz practiced with all of us and helped us build the confidence we needed to have a voice while accepting that we sounded different than the other students in the school.

By the end of the 8th grade I was much better at reading and speaking English. To celebrate our accomplishments, Ms. Gershowitz held a pool party at her house for the six of us and our families. She praised the great work we had done in her class that year and encouraged our parents to have us speak English as much as possible over the summer so we would be ready for high school. I spent only 1 year with Ms. Gershowitz, but the friendships I built and the lessons I learned have lingered. I learned to forgive myself if I failed at something and to try again and again, until I mastered the skill. I learned to believe in my ability to succeed even when others do not believe I will, and to love being Afro-Latinx, bilingual, an unapologetic *Boricua*. I also learned to be compassionate to others who faced similar struggles to be seen by blind educators. From 9th grade on, I focused on debunking the prejudiced limitations placed on me by others, by always being in competition with myself. I loved school and I love being an educator, but my story may have turned out totally different were it not for two extraordinary teachers who saw my worth and taught me the lessons I needed to learn to succeed in school and in life. To them, I will be forever grateful.

RECOMMENDATIONS FOR PRESERVICE AND INSERVICE TEACHER DEVELOPMENT

Revisiting my academic experiences and framing my reflections on critical race theory and Latinx critical theory, I offer the following recommendations for preservice and inservice teacher development and personal practices:

1. Consider how stereotypes, prejudices, and biases intentionality may be showing up in your classroom. Reflect on how your tone, student–teacher relationships, classroom policies, and discipline practices differ between students of color and other students, and consider how these behaviors and practices hinder learning opportunities for your students of color (Stein et al., 2018). Take corrective action to make your approach more equitable and culturally and linguistically responsive.
2. Cultivate intentional and authentic relationships with ELLs adjusting to U.S. schools to promote positive experiences (Newcomer, 2018) that will keep students engaged in formal education and prevent widening the achievement gap and school dropouts.

3. Promote student engagement by using literature that reflects students' cultures, lives, and school experiences to awaken consciousness and advocacy (Huerta, 2011).

CONCLUSION

I became a Special Education teacher to give to my students what my teachers had given to me: love, compassion, self-acceptance, and self-worth. My students learned that they mattered to me and that I believed they could excel in my class despite the limitations that others placed on them. I taught self-contained high school math for 7 years and helped my students, many of whom were Black and Latinx, to graduate from high school with a diploma, by awakening in them a sense of optimism. My students were rejected by many of my fellow teachers. However, with love, patience, and compassion, I was able to rebuild their confidence. Now as a school principal, I continue to work with students with exceptionalities and English Language Learners, and I empower my teachers to have an outward mindset, to discover the abilities of our students, and to discredit ableism. The measure of success for my teachers is not whether the students learn to read, write, or count. It is for my teachers to discontinue the practice of underserving and marginalizing students of color and establish bonds that help our students feel safe and encouraged to try to work harder.

The point of education is learning, not teaching. The lessons I learned from Ms. Tapia and Ms. Gershowitz were not taught, they were learned by the experiences I had engaging them socially and emotionally. Their examples and explanations framed how I approached schooling, regardless of who was "teaching" me. Had they only focused on the content and not the student, I would not have learned those lessons and would not have had the privilege to pass them on to my students and my staff. Thus I urge every teacher, new or seasoned, to focus their lens on the students and to help them learn imperative lessons like forgiveness, discipline, grit, optimism, and many others that focus on empowering the child to become a successful learner of the most important subject: self-worth.

REFERENCES

American School Counselor Association (ASCA). (2003). *Position statement: Family/parenting education.* https://apsa.org/sites/default/files/2012%20%20Position%20Statement%20on%20Parenting.pdf

Benner, A. D., & Graham, S. (2011). Latino adolescents' experiences of discrimination across the first 2 years of high school: Correlates and influences on educational outcomes. *Child Development, 82*(2), 508–519. https://doi.org/10.1111/j.1467-8624.2010.01524.x

Bonilla-Silva, E. (2017). *Racism without racists: Color-blind racism and the persistence of racial inequality in America.* Rowman & Littlefield.

Delpit, L. (1995). *Other people's children: Cultural conflict in the classroom.* The New Press.

Ellis, A. L. (2019). Foreword: Leveraging empirical research: Storytelling among Black educational leaders. In R. T. Palmer, M. O. Cadet, K. Le-Niles, & J. L. Hughes (Eds.), *Personal narratives of Black educational leaders: Pathways to academic success* (pp. vii–x). Routledge.

Ferlazzo, L. (2006). Response: How to practice restorative justice in schools. *Classroom Q&A with Larry Ferlazzo(Blog), Education Week Teacher.* https://blogs.edweek.org/teachers/classroom_qa_with_larry_ferlazzo/2016/02/response_how_to_practice_restorative_justice_in_schools.html

Freire, P. (1972). *Pedagogy of the oppressed.* Herder and Herder. (Original work published 1968)

Gitlin, A., Buendia, E., Crosland, K., & Doumbia, F. (2003). The production of margin and center: Welcoming–unwelcoming of immigrant students. *American Educational Research Journal, 40*(1), 91–122. https://doi.org/10.3102/00028312040001091

Harklau, L. (2000). From the "good kids" to the "worst": Representations of English language learners across educational settings. *TESOL Quarterly, 34,* 35–67. https://doi.org/10.2307/3588096

Huerta, T. M. (2011). Humanizing pedagogy: Beliefs and practices on the teaching of Latino children, *Bilingual Research Journal, 34*(1), 38–57. https://doi.org/10.1080/15235882.2011.568826

Ladson-Billings, G. (1995). But that's just good teaching! The case for culturally relevant pedagogy. *Theory Into Practice, 34*(3), 159–165.

Lewis, L., Parsad, B., Carey, N., Bartfai, N., Farris, E., & Smerdon, B. (1999). *Teacher quality: A report on the preparation and qualifications of public school teachers* [NCES 1999-080]. U.S. Department of Education, Institute of Education Sciences, National Center for Education Statistics. Available for download from https://nces.ed.gov/pubsearch/pubsinfo.asp?pubid=1999080

Lewis, T. J., Hudson, S., Richter, M., & Johnson, N. (2004). Scientifically supported practices in emotional and behavioral disorders: A proposed approach and brief review of current practices. *Behavioral Disorders, 29*(3), 247–259. https://doi.org/10.1177/019874290402900306

McKerchar, P. M., & Thompson, R. H. (2004). A descriptive analysis of potential reinforcement contingencies in the preschool classroom. *Journal of Applied Behavior Analysis, 37*(4), 431–444.

Moore Partin, T. C., Robertson, R. E., Maggin, D. M., Oliver, R. M., & Wehby, J. H. (2009). Using teacher praise and opportunities to respond to promote appropriate student behavior. *Preventing School Failure: Alternative Education for Children and Youth, 54*(3), 172–178. https://doi.org/10.1080/10459880903493179

National Center for Education Statistics. (2019). *Spotlight A: Characteristics of public school teachers by race/ethnicity.* https://nces.ed.gov/programs/raceindicators/spotlight_a.asp

Newcomer, S. N. (2018). Investigating the power of authentically caring student–teacher relationships for Latinx students. *Journal of Latinos and Education, 17*(2), 179–193. https://doi.org/10.1080/15348431.2017.1310104

Olsen, L. (1997). *Made in America: Immigrant students in our public schools.* The New Press.

Platt, E., Harper, C., & Mendoza, M. B. (2003). Dueling philosophies: Inclusion or separation for Florida's English language learners? *TESOL Quarterly, 37*(1), 105–133. https://doi.org/10.2307/3588467

Reeves, J. (2004). "Like everybody else": Equalizing educational opportunity for English language learners. *TESOL Quarterly, 38*(1), 43–66

Schmidt, M. A. (2000). Teachers' attitudes toward ESL students and programs. In S. Wade (Ed.), *Inclusive education: A casebook and readings for prospective and practicing teachers* (pp. 121–128). Erlbaum.

Skiba, R. J., Horner, R. H., Chung, C.-G., Rausch, M. K., May, S. L., & Tobin, T. (2011). Race is not neutral: A national investigation of African American and Latino disproportionality in school discipline. *School Psychology Review, 40*(1), 85–107. https://doi.org/10.1080/02796015.2011.12087730

Stein, K. C., Wright, J., Gil, E., Miness, A., & Ginanto, D. (2018). Examining Latina/o students' experiences of injustice: LatCrit insights from a Texas high school. *Journal of Latinos and Education, 17*(2), 103–120. https://doi.org/10.1080/15348431.2017.1282367

Valdes, G. (2001). *Learning and not learning English: Latino students in American schools.* Teachers College Press.

Verplaetse, L. (1998). How content interact with English Language Learners. *TESOL Journal, 7*(5), 24-28.

Vollmer, G. (2000). Praise and stigma: Teachers' constructions of the "typical ESL student." *Journal of Intercultural Studies 21*(1), 53–66.

Walqui, A. (2000). *Access and engagement: Program design and instructional approaches for immigrant students in secondary schools.* Center for Applied Linguistics.

Wubbels, T., Brekelmans, M., van Tartwijk, J., & Admiraal, W. (1999). Interpersonal relationships between teachers and students in the classroom. In H. C. Waxman & H. J. Walberg (Eds.), *New directions for teaching practice and research* (pp. 151– 170). McCutchan.

Youngs, C. S. (1999). *Mainstreaming the marginalized: Secondary mainstream teachers' perceptions of ESL students* (Publication No. 679) [Doctoral dissertation, University of North Dakota]. UND Scholarly Commons, Theses and Dissertations. https://commons.und.edu/theses/679/

The Deliberative Practice of Teacher Educators' Reflections on Culturally Relevant Teachers

This book is a compilation of writings by accomplished educators, education researchers, and educational leaders providing their powerful narratives of effective teachers: both familial and professional.

It begins by paying homage to the seminal text written by Gloria Ladson-Billings, *The Dreamkeepers: Successful Teachers of African American Children,* and then acknowledges those educators that have kept the dream of prosperity through education pervasive and alive. One can only believe that the strong teachers cited in their upbringing have played a pivotal role in developing the scholarship produced by these acclaimed leaders. The authors of this text are educators and scholars who have studied the patterns of American education and assessed it through mirrors and windows. The phrase "mirrors and windows" was initially introduced by Emily Style, founding codirector of the National SEED Project. A *mirror* is a story and style of pedagogy that reflects a student's culture and helps to build and understand their identity. A *window* is a portrayal that offers you a view into someone else's lived experience. Education is much more than knowledge transmission. Obviously, a combination of the two pedagogical resources are needed in the toolkit of culturally relevant teachers, as windows and mirrors emphasize the need for students to learn about themselves as well as others.

In this inspirational mixture of scholarship and storytelling, the authors in this collection articulate and illustrate ways that their teachers were able to hold them to high standards while acknowledging their strengths or gifts. In many cases their teachers were able to create the opportunity to learn in the absence of optimism. Each chapter is a constant reminder and affirmation of the importance of critical pedagogy, where social change is linked to education. These narrative or ethnographic accounts frame their personal reflexive views of the self where their data are situated within their lived experiences.

The posthumous recognition of educators such as Mary McCloud Bethune alongside parents and everyday classroom teachers, have affirmatively shaped the authors and their epistemological view of the education system. They have acknowledged the weighted contribution that these unsung heroes had on their lives. Many of these stories included some affiliation or connection to HBCUs. This comes as no surprise since HBCUs have played such a significant role in training Black teachers and building the Black middle class.

I am reminded of my pathway to become an educator. People often are surprised to hear that as a student in the NYC Public Schools, I had no Black teachers. Because of that lack of diverse academic representation, I enrolled at an HBCU. There I learned and felt the benefits of a culturally affirming education. However, my first informal role as a teacher was by the invitation of a Black kindergarten teacher when I was in 3rd grade. She asked for me and a classmate to come to her class twice a week to grade papers and work with small groups of students. This unforgettable experience provided a glimpse of the intrinsic rewards that are often felt by teachers.

Students of color comprise more than half of the student population in public elementary and secondary schools; however, teachers of color represent approximately 20% of the teaching force. Despite research showing the benefits of a diverse teaching staff for all students, we have not adequately diversified our nation's teaching force. Adding to this dynamic is research that shows that teachers of color provide more culturally relevant instruction and develop stronger rapport with students of color. They also hold more positive expectations of students of color compared to their White counterparts. Clearly, schools must make diversifying the teaching force a primary goal, but they must go further—they must change the way educators teach students of color by incorporating culturally affirming strategies that have demonstrated success for traditionally marginalized student populations. Many of these strategies are repeated in multiple personal accounts in this text.

We have seen what appears to be a linear progression toward the inclusion of culture in teaching and learning. From the era of teaching tolerance, to cultural relevance, to now cultural responsiveness, each more progressive than the last, we have worked to transform pedagogical techniques to better meet the needs of students that have historically been underserved. Many of these movements were introduced by scholars within the discipline of educator preparation. It is where the next generation of educators are trained and best represents the future of the profession. As schools are the epitome of learning organizations, we should be open to the insistence of continuous improvement to reach these goals.

We have been provided a roadmap from scholars such as Gloria Ladson-Billings, A. Wade Boykin, Donna Ford, Linda Darling Hammond, and others to build and foster an environment that inspires inquiry and discovery, and honors educators as facilitators. This roadmap describes the importance of being student-centered, learning within the context of culture, communicating high expectations, and having positive perspectives of parents and families.

Culturally affirming practices advance this movement from efforts of acknowledgment to proactive efforts of empowerment. This requires a level of appreciation and not just tolerance. This appreciation should be visible to students of all backgrounds. This looks like educators working to understand, respect, and meet the needs of students who come from culturally diverse backgrounds. It requires the enthusiastic inclusion of parents, families, and the cultural community at large. Alongside the community at large, educators will coconstruct critically reflective learning experiences for the purpose of achieving academic success and positive identity development.

While the adoption of culturally affirming practices and pedagogy has great significance in culturally diverse schools, it also holds value for schools in which the student population is majority White. All students need to see educators embrace the appreciation and affirmation of our diverse society, even if that diversity is not present in their classrooms. This expression of inclusion provides a more just presentation of our democratic society in which our youth will eventually participate. Students of all racial backgrounds can benefit from a diverse teacher workforce and a culturally affirming curriculum that represents the nation's overall demographics.

At the time of this publication, we are in the midst of a global health pandemic: the coronavirus. The rapid spread of the coronavirus has forced all schools (elementary through postsecondary) in the country to close for months. It has necessitated distant learning and remote instruction. Every sector of the society is feeling the impact of this virus, but these effects are hardest among those who were already most vulnerable. The inequities in our country are being magnified by the masses and are most visible in our education system. The pandemic has brought greater attention to the disparities among racial and economic groups. It has magnified just how uneven the playing field is. Herein lies an opportunity to rebuild an education system that does not include structural deficits, but does include the positive pedagogical strategies cited throughout this text.

Mark Twain once stated, "History doesn't repeat itself, but it often rhymes." We cannot afford to experience déjà vu and double down on the now layered inequities in schools. Texts like *Teacher Educators as Critical Storytellers: Effective Teachers as Windows and Mirrors* aid in increasing our awareness and understanding in order to address factors that contribute to inequities. We all have a critical role to play in dismantling ineffective structures and coconstructing affirming educational spaces.

—Dawn G. Williams
Professor and Dean
Howard University School of Education

About the Editors and the Contributors

THE EDITORS

Antonio L. Ellis, EdD, is scholar in residence and director of the Institute on Education Equity and Justice at the American University School of Education. In addition, Ellis is Manager of Specialized Instruction with the District of Columbia Public Schools. His research focuses on critical race theory in special education with an emphasis on African American male students who are speech impaired.

Nicholas D. Hartlep, PhD, is the Robert Charles Billings Endowed Chair in Education at Berea College where he chairs the Department of Education Studies. Before coming to Berea College Hartlep chaired the Department of Early Childhood and Elementary Education at Metropolitan State University, an Asian American and Native American Pacific Islander-Serving Institution (AANAPISI) in St. Paul, Minnesota. While there he also served as Graduate Program Coordinator. Hartlep has published 23 books, the most recent one about teaching and learning is *What Makes a Star Teacher? Seven Dispositions That Encourage Student Learning,* published by the Association for Supervision and Curriculum Development in 2019. His book *The Neoliberal Agenda and the Student Debt Crisis in U.S. Higher Education,* coedited with Lucille L. T. Eckrich and Brandon O. Hensley in 2017, was named an Outstanding Book by the Society of Professors of Education. Hartlep has received numerous awards. Most recently, the American Association for Access, Equity, and Diversity (AAAED) honored him with the 2020 Emerging Leader Award; and *Diverse: Issues in Higher Education* named him an Emerging Scholar in 2019. Previous awards include: in 2018, the John Saltmarsh Award for Emerging Leaders in Civic Engagement from the Association of State Colleges and Universities (AASCU); in 2017, the Community Engaged Scholarship Award and the President's

Circle of Engagement Award from Metropolitan State University; in 2016, a Graduate of the Last Decade Award for his prolific writing from the University of Wisconsin–Milwaukee; in 2015, the University Research Initiative Award from Illinois State University and a Distinguished Young Alumni Award from Winona State University.

Gloria Ladson-Billings, PhD, is professor emerita and former Kellner Family Distinguished Chair of Urban Education at the University of Wisconsin–Madison. She is president of the National Academy of Education (NAEd) and a fellow of the American Academy of Arts & Sciences (AAAS).

David O. Stovall, PhD, is a professor of African American Studies and Criminology, Law, and Justice at the University of Illinois–Chicago. His research interests lie at the intersection of race, place, school, and the abolition of the school–prison nexus.

THE CONTRIBUTORS

Judy Alston, PhD, is a professor as well as the director of the EdD in Leadership Studies program in the Department of Doctoral Studies and Advanced Programs at Ashland University. She earned her PhD in Educational Administration from The Pennsylvania State University, an MDiv from Methodist Theological School in Ohio, an MEd in Educational Administration and an MEd in Secondary Education from the University of South Carolina, and a BA in English from Winthrop College. An educator for over 30 years, she is a prolific author, speaker, and presenter. She is the author of many articles, book chapters, and books including *Herstories: Leading with the Lessons of the Lives of Black Women Activists; Multi-leadership in Urban Schools;* and *School Leadership and Administration: Important Concepts, Case Studies, & Simulations* (7th–10th eds.). Her research foci include Black female school superintendents; the exploration of how the intersections of class, race, ethnicity, gender, sexuality, and ability affect leaders; tempered radicals and refined revolutionaries; servant leadership; spirituality; and Black LGBTQ+ issues in leadership.

Roslyn Clark Artis, EdD, is the 14th and first female president in the 147-year history of Benedict College. Artis came to Benedict College from Florida Memorial University, where she served for 4 years as the 13th and first female president in that university's 138-year history. Intentional, professional, and thoroughly committed to the proliferation and transformation of colleges and universities that serve underrepresented men and women of color, Artis brings a depth of knowledge in higher education and enthusiasm for students' success that is unmatched in today's higher education arena. She has led a remarkable institutional transformation that included lowering tuition, increasing academic standards, stabilizing the institution's financial position, streamlining academic degree programs, and upgrading the institution's technology infrastructure. A prolific speaker, critical thinker, and fierce advocate for educational access, Artis has been recognized for her work locally and nationally and is frequently engaged as a mentor, lecturer, and catalyst for strategic transformation.

Aimeé I. Cepeda, EdD, is an urban school leader who advocates for students furthest from opportunities, specifically students with disabilities and English language learners (ELLs). Cepeda holds a doctoral degree in Educational Leadership and Policy Studies from Howard University, an MS in Special Education from The Johns Hopkins University, and a BS in Computer Sciences from Strayer University. Additionally, she is soon to complete a post-doctoral Certificate in Advanced Education Leadership from the Harvard University Graduate School of Education. Cepeda is passionate about challenging the idea of incongruent education for general education students, students with exceptionalities, and ELLs with the hopes of finding creative solutions to eradicate this system of triality. Her research interests are critical race theory and Latinx critical theory in special education and English as a second language instruction.

Theodore Chao, PhD, is an assistant professor of Mathematics Education in the Department of Teaching and Learning at The Ohio State University. His research agenda involves engaging all students and teachers regardless of social identity (race, gender, socioeconomic status, and so on) to fully see themselves as mathematical humans, particularly through technology. He uses Digital Storytelling and Photovoice as vehicles for mathematics teachers and students of color to create narratives that connect their mathematics identities with their community and family identities. He also builds technology for children to share their mathematical strategies, opening up windows for peers, teachers, and family members to recognize the brilliance of their mathematical thinking. Chao has published in journals such as *Investigations* *in Mathematics Learning; Race, Ethnicity, and Education;* and *Teaching Children Mathematics.* He is currently the principal investigator of an NSF CAREER research project exploring the ways children in urban emergent communities use Digital Mathematics Storytelling to share rich mathematical knowledge from their communities and families. Chao has taught courses such as Elementary Mathematics Methods, A Critical History of STEM Education, and Mobile App Development in STEM Education. He is currently an associate editor for *Theory Into Practice (TIP)*, an editorial panel member of *Mathematics Teacher Educator (MTE)*, a steering committee member of the North American Chapter of the International Group for the Psychology of Mathematics Education (PME-NA), and an organizer for the Free Minds, Free People (FMFP) conference.

Ramon B. Goings, EdD, is an assistant professor in the Language, Literacy, and Culture interdisciplinary doctoral program at the University of Maryland–Baltimore County (UMBC). His research examines gifted and high-achieving Black male academic success pre-K–PhD, diversifying the teacher and school leader workforce, and the student experience and contributions of historically Black colleges and universities to the higher education landscape.

Lisa Maria Grillo, EdD, is an assistant professor and doctoral coordinator in the Department of Educational Leadership and Policy Studies in the Howard University School of Education, where she conducts research regarding the experiences of women of color in educational leadership. Prior to this, Grillo was a teacher, school administrator, and district leader for 23 years, where she successfully led district- and school-level initiatives in large urban and suburban school districts.

Jameson D. Lopez, PhD, is an assistant professor in the Center for the Study of Higher Education at the University of Arizona. He is an enrolled member of the Quechan tribe located in Fort Yuma, California. Lopez studies Native American education using Indigenous statistics and has expertise in the limitations of collecting and applying quantitative results to Indigenous populations. He carries unique experiences to his research that include a 2010 deployment to Iraq as a platoon leader where he received a Bronze Star Medal for actions in a combat zone. Most importantly, he is a proud father of two beautiful children, Luna and Gordon.

Shawn Anthony Robinson, PhD, is a senior researcher associate in Wisconsin's Equity and Inclusion Laboratory (Wei LAB) and an instructional program manager in the Department of Rehabilitation Psychology and Special Education at the University of Wisconsin–Madison. Robinson is a dyslexia consultant, whose research focuses on the intersection of giftedness and dyslexia, and writes about African American males with dyslexia. He brings a wealth of academic and personal experience, training, and knowledge about the development of dyslexia.

Theresa Stewart-Ambo, PhD (member of the Tongva/Luiseño/Tohono O'odham tribes) is an assistant professor in the Department of Education Studies at the University of California–San Diego (Kumeyaay territory). She holds a bachelor's, master's, and doctoral degree in Education from the University of California–Los Angeles (Tongva territory). From 2017–2019, Stewart-Ambo was a University of California President's Postdoctoral Fellow at UC–San Diego. Theresa's research focuses on issues related to American Indian educational equity and inclusion, including student outcomes and community–campus partnerships. Her research examines historic and contemporary relationships between public universities and local tribal nations in California, offering institutionally transferable insights and frameworks on "tribal–university relationships" to address tribal sovereignty and self-determination.

Amanda R. Tachine, PhD is an assistant professor in Educational Leadership and Innovation at Arizona State University, where she advances ideas and strategies to increase Native college student success. Amanda was recognized by President Barack Obama with the White House Champions of Change: Young Women Empowering Communities award for her instrumental work in creating University of Arizona's Native Student Outreach for Access and Resiliency (SOAR). She has published thought pieces in the *Huffington Post, Al Jazeera, The Hill, Teen Vogue, Indian Country Today, Inside Higher Ed*, and *Navajo Times* in which she advances ideas regarding discriminatory actions, educational policies, and inspirational movements.

Index